Ghost Buster's Guide: The Truth Behind Paranormal Claims

Myrddin Sage

Published by Myrddin Sage, 2024.

GHOST BUSTER'S GUIDE: THE TRUTH BEHIND PARANORMAL CLAIMS

First edition. September 30, 2024.

ISBN: 979-8227645821

Written by Myrddin Sage.

To the seekers of truth and the brave souls who dare to question the unknown. This guide is for those who walk the fine line between skepticism and belief, and for the countless spirits, real or imagined, who inspire our quest for understanding. May this journey through the shadows bring clarity, courage, and a touch of wonder to all who embark upon it.

Ghost Buster's Guide: Unveiling the Truth Behind Paranormal Claims

Master the Art of Paranormal Investigation with Scientific Insight and Skepticism in Just Weeks

Preface

"All truths are easy to understand once they are discovered; the point is to discover them." - Galileo Galilei.

This book seeks to explore and uncover the truth behind paranormal claims in the mysterious twilight realm, where whispers and moving shadows blur the line between reality and fiction. It is designed for those fascinated by ghost stories and haunted tales but also approaches them with skepticism and a desire for scientific inquiry.

My journey to write this book began one crisp autumn evening when a close friend shared his unsettling experience at an old, supposedly haunted hotel. His story was filled with unexplained noises and a chilling encounter that left him sleepless for nights.

However, what struck me the most was his frustration at not finding a rational explanation for his experiences that night. This incident and many letters from others facing similar dilemmas inspired me to create a resource that demystifies the paranormal through logic and scientific principles. In making this guide, I drew inspiration from various fields and experts, including psychologists, historians, and seasoned paranormal investigators, whose insights have been invaluable. I extend my heartfelt gratitude to every reader who has delved into this book. Your curiosity and willingness to engage with this subject breathe life into these pages.

This book promises to equip you with the tools to investigate and rationalize paranormal claims, transforming fear into understanding. This guide is intended for amateur ghost hunters, fans of mystery and thriller genres, and skeptics seeking a grounded perspective on supernatural occurrences. No prior expertise in psychology or paranormal studies is required—just an open mind and a keen interest in separating fact from fiction.

I invite you to journey through this book with an open mind, a heart, and a questioning mind. Let's explore the unknown, challenge preconceived notions, and change how we perceive the world.

Thank you for bringing your enthusiasm and curiosity into this exploration. Let's turn the page and begin this intriguing voyage toward understanding the mysterious phenomena that captivate our imaginations and stir our fears.

Chapter 1: Spirits of the Afterlife: Myth or Science?

Can Ghosts Speak Through the Veil of Death?

On a crisp autumn evening in the small town of Eldridge, nestled between rolling hills and shadowed by ancient oaks, Margaret walked down Main Street. The leaves rustled under her feet, whispering secrets of the past as they crunched in a symphony of reds and golds. She pulled her coat tighter against the chill that fought through her layers and seemed to seep into her bones—a cold that felt almost spectral.

Margaret had lived in Eldridge all her life, a town famous for its ghost stories and unexplained phenomena. As a child, she listened wide-eyed to tales of spirits wandering through the town at night, searching for something or someone they had left behind. Now, as an adult, she couldn't help but feel those stories tugging at her with more insistence. Her father had passed away recently, leaving behind a house filled with memories and an unshakable sense of his presence.

She stopped in front of the old library, a building as much part of her childhood as any living friend. Its stone façade held firm against time's relentless march, its windows reflecting the setting sun like watching eyes. Inside was where she first learned about ghosts—not just the tales from Eldridge but what scientists said about them: figments of imagination or dreaming by those who grieved.

As she entered through the creaking doors, greeted by the familiar musty smell mixed with old books and leather-bound histories, Margaret thought about how these walls once made her feel safe.

Now they housed questions she wasn't sure she wanted answered.

Her footsteps echoed off high ceilings adorned with frescoes fading like old memories. She wandered through stacks until she found what she sought: books on paranormal research and scientific inquiries into life after death. The librarian watched her curiously from across the room—everyone knew everyone here—and perhaps wondered what drove Margaret to these dusty shelves.

Sitting at a carved wooden table beneath a flickering light bulb that struggled to keep the darkness at bay outside its small circle of influence, Margaret flipped through pages filled with skepticism and rational explanations for hauntings. Each word weighed heavy on her heart, and stillness enveloped her like a shroud.

Could science indeed disprove what countless people had experienced? Could it erase the sound of steps in an empty room upstairs or explain away cold spots in a home warmed by fireplaces and love? How could it contend with the feeling of being watched when alone or decipher dreams where dead loved ones appeared so vividly?

Margaret sighs deeply—the kind that felt like surrender—and whispered into the surrounding quiet: "Are you here?"

Outside, another leaf fell silent to join its fellows on their last journey across stone paths worn smooth by generations walking between belief and disbelief—both haunted in their ways.

Could some mysteries remain beyond our understanding?

Is Your Haunted House Just a House?

When we hear bumps in the night or witness shadows flicker from the corner of our eyes, our minds often jump to a haunting explanation: ghosts. That spirits of the dead linger among us is both terrifying and fascinating, deeply ingrained in our cultural narratives and personal fears. But what if there's more to these stories? What if our understanding of these eerie encounters is clouded by myth rather than illuminated by evidence?

Throughout this guide, we delve deep into the heart of what many call the paranormal, but with a twist—armed with skepticism and scientific inquiry. This first chapter sets the stage for a journey that challenges conventional ghost narratives and invites you to look beyond the tales that have thrilled and chilled humanity for generations.

Understanding Ghosts: More Than Just Stories?

Ghosts, as traditionally depicted, are believed to be the spirits of those who've passed away, somehow anchored to the world of the living. This concept thrives in whispered legends, horror films, and countless personal anecdotes where individuals swear by their spectral encounters. However, despite the prevalence of these beliefs, **a critical examination reveals a stark lack of scientific evidence supporting these claims.** Our exploration here is not to discount personal experiences but to question and analyze them through a scientific lens.

The persistence of ghost stories raises essential questions about why these beliefs are so widespread despite the absence of empirical support. Could our brains be wired to perceive more than what meets the eye under certain conditions? Or perhaps there's comfort in thinking our loved ones remain close by, watching over us even after death.

The Science Behind the Spirits

As we discuss this further, it's crucial to separate anecdote from analysis. Parapsychology has long attempted to study what many claim to be evidence of the afterlife.

Yet, rigorous scientific methods—replicable and controlled experiments—have consistently failed to validate the existence of ghosts. This chapter will explore how psychological factors, environmental influences, and electromagnetic fields can be mistaken for paranormal activity.

By encouraging a skeptical approach to supernatural claims, we aim to debunk myths and prevent the spread of misinformation that can often lead to unnecessary fear or exploitation. It's about empowering you with knowledge and critical thinking skills to dissect the real from the unreal in the shadows of uncertainty.

Tools for Tomorrow's Ghost Hunters

Readers who understand what ghosts aren't will be ready to learn how to investigate claims of hauntings effectively.

This book promises tools for debunking and understanding human perception and its fallibilities. By mastering these skills, you can approach any claim—paranormal or otherwise—with a healthy balance of skepticism and openness.

This journey through "Ghost Buster's Guide" is designed not just as an exploration of paranormal phenomena but also as an educational course on critical thinking and scientific inquiry—skills that are vital far beyond any haunted house.

With each page turned, let us challenge old fears with new insights and transform curiosity into knowledge. Let this be more than just a hunt for ghosts; it is a quest for truth amidst tales as old as time.

Whether you're a staunch skeptic or a willing believer, there's much here for everyone to learn about what lurks in the unseen spaces—not just in haunted halls but in the corners of our minds waiting to be illuminated by reason.

Understanding the Popular Conception of Ghosts as Spirits of the Deceased

The idea that ghosts are the spirits of the deceased has been a staple of folklore and cultural stories worldwide. From the ancient Egyptian belief in the Ka, or spirit double, to the Victorian era's fascination with séances, the notion that the dead can communicate with the living has captivated human imagination for centuries.

That read belief is often rooted in the desire for continuity beyond physical death, offering comfort and a sense of connection to lost loved ones.

However, when we peel back the layers of these stories, we find a tapestry woven with threads of hope and fear. Imagine if memories were like old letters stored in an attic—ghost stories are the dust we blow off these letters, hoping to reconnect with the past. In many cultures, these tales also serve as moral lessons or warnings, shaping social norms and behaviors.

Scientifically, there has been no verifiable evidence that supports these beliefs as factual. Investigations into paranormal activities often rely heavily on anecdotal evidence and personal testimonies, which do not meet the stringent requirements of scientific methodology. The tools used in these investigations, from EMF meters to voice recorders, have not conclusively proven the existence of ghosts.

Despite lacking scientific evidence, the belief in ghosts persists, highlighting a broader aspect of human psychology. Our brains are pattern-seeking machines, and in the face of unexplainable occurrences, they often default to the most culturally and emotionally satisfying explanation. This psychological aspect underscores the enduring appeal of ghost stories and the idea of an afterlife.

The popular conception of ghosts as spirits of the deceased continues to thrive, not because of scientific validation but because of its deep roots in human culture and psychology.

Examining the Lack of Scientific Evidence for Human Consciousness After Death

The quest to understand consciousness and its potential survival after physical death has intrigued scientists and philosophers alike.

Despite extensive research in neuroscience and related fields, no scientific evidence suggests that consciousness can persist after the brain stops functioning. The brain is an immensely complex organ, and consciousness is believed to arise from its electrochemical interactions.

Scientists have used advanced imaging techniques to study the brain's activity during life. Still, these studies cease to show activity once life ends. The cessation of brain function typically marks the end of consciousness as we understand it. Here, it's essential to distinguish between resuscitation cases, where individuals have reported near-death experiences (NDEs), and actual death. While profoundly affecting and honest with those who experience them, NDEs do not provide empirical evidence of consciousness existing independently of the brain.

Efforts to scientifically verify the paranormal have consistently fallen short. Paranormal investigations often involve methodologies that are not replicable or controlled, leading to subjective interpretations of the data. This lack of rigor makes it difficult to draw reliable conclusions from such studies.

It's akin to trying to listen to a radio broadcast without a radio; we can wish and believe there's a signal, but without the proper equipment (in this case, a functioning brain), receiving that signal is impossible. This analogy helps illustrate why scientific proof remains elusive despite the desire to believe in life after death.

Could the absence of concrete evidence make us reconsider our understanding of life and death?

Encouraging Critical Analysis of Paranormal Claims Related to Spirits

Critical thinking is essential when examining claims of the paranormal. By applying a skeptical and analytical approach, individuals can distinguish between evidence-based conclusions and those founded on anecdotal or subjective experiences. This process involves scrutinizing the methods used to gather evidence and the interpretations of that evidence.

For instance, consider a typical ghost hunting show. The investigators might use electronic devices that they claim detect ghostly presences. However, with a clear understanding of how these devices work and what exactly they're measuring, it's easier to understand natural environmental factors as paranormal activity.

Human perception is highly susceptible to suggestion. In environments where ghostly encounters are expected, people are more likely to perceive ordinary occurrences—such as a draft or a creaking floor—as supernatural. This psychological phenomenon, known as pareidolia, occurs when the mind responds to a stimulus (usually an image or a sound) by perceiving a familiar pattern where none exists.

One could employ a simple framework to critically analyze such claims: observe, question, and test. Observing involves looking at the evidence presented and noting all explanations. Questioning is about probing more deeply into how the conclusions were drawn.

Testing involves seeking replicable, controlled experiments to confirm or debunk the claims.

By understanding the popular conception of ghosts, examining the scientific evidence, and employing critical thinking, we better equip ourselves to navigate the intriguing world of paranormal claims. This comprehensive approach enriches our understanding and sharpens our analytical skills, which apply to all areas of life.

Through the pages of this chapter, we've embarked on a journey to demystify the enigmatic concept of ghosts as spirits of the deceased. We've scrutinized **the popular narratives** that entwine our cultural and personal landscapes, enriching our understanding but also challenging our credulity. Our exploration revealed a significant gap: the *absence of scientific evidence* to support the notion that human consciousness persists after death in any form that interacts with the living.

Reflecting on these findings encourages us to question and apply rigorous **critical analysis** to paranormal claims. This analytical mindset isn't just about debunking myths; it's a profound commitment to understanding reality, enhancing our grasp on the natural world, and fostering a healthy skepticism that shields us from deception.

The insights gained here are merely the beginning. As you continue this book, each chapter will build on the last, equipping you with robust scientific tools and skeptical inquiry techniques. You will learn not just to question the existence of the paranormal but to analyze evidence, differentiate between assertion and fact, and, ultimately, make informed conclusions grounded in scientific methodology.

Embrace this knowledge as both a shield and a beacon: a shield against the allure of unverified claims and guiding you toward enlightened understanding. The journey into the paranormal is as thrilling as it is enlightening, and the skills you develop will serve you well beyond the realm of spirits and specters.

Prepare to challenge your preconceptions, push the boundaries of your understanding, and discover the exciting world of paranormal investigation. This is not just about ghosts—it's about nurturing a keen, questioning mind that enhances every aspect of your life. Let's continue this adventure with open eyes and minds ready to learn.

Chapter 2: The Psychological Shadows of Haunted Places

Can a Place Remember Tragedy?

Thomas stood in the heart of Edinburgh under a sky smeared with twilight colors. He was a rational man, bound to the earth by logic and evidence, yet here he was at the gates of Mary King's Close, a place heavy with whispers of the past. The chill in the air was from the Scottish breeze and the stories embedded in the cobblestones and walls—tales of plague victims sealed away to die.

Thomas rubbed his hands together, not just for warmth but in a nervous gesture that belied his usual composure. He remembered his grandmother's tales, spun like webs around old tragedies and spectral figures seen only in the corner of one's eye. As a child, these stories were thrilling; as an adult, they were curious relics of psychological landscapes.

He stepped forward, his shoes echoing on the ancient stones. The echo seemed to carry more than sound—it vibrated with history, with sorrow. It was said that expectations shaped perceptions in places like this. Thomas knew this intellectually but felt something else—an itch at the back of his neck that wasn't entirely self-made.

Inside Mary King's Close, shadows clung to corners like cobwebs. The dim light played tricks on eyes too eager to see something unexplainable. Thomas paused in a small room where children's laughter could sometimes be heard, though no children had played there for centuries. He closed his eyes briefly, straining against reason to listen.

A tour guide's voice broke through his concentration, recounting grim histories with theatrical flair. "And here," she pointed to a darker corner of the room, "is where many claim to feel sudden drops in temperature or unexplained sadness." The surrounding group shuffled closer together as if proximity could shield them from unseen forces.

As Thomas listened to her stories interwoven with facts and folklore, he was caught between two worlds—the seen and the unseen: what is known and what is felt. His mind wrestled with dismissive explanations even as goosebumps formed on his arms under layers of clothing.

Was it merely human nature to seek patterns in randomness? To attribute eerie feelings to spirits rather than psychology? As he stepped out into less shadowed corridors, he pondered how much weight should be given to an atmosphere influenced by tragic histories versus logical explanations grounded in science.

As the night deepened its hold over Edinburgh and lights twinkled like stars fallen onto cobbled streets below him, Thomas strolled back towards modernity. Still, he carried an age-old question: When we stand in places steeped in sorrow or tragedy, can we ever truly be observers unaffected by their histories?

Are You Seeing Ghosts or Just Seeing What You Expect to See?

When you step into a place known for its ghostly encounters, what influences the chills that creep up your spine? Is it the cold draft meandering through the broken windows, or could it be the eerie tales whispered about the old mansion at the town's edge? This chapter delves into the intriguing interplay between a location's sad history and the psychological effects it can exert on those who dare to visit. Our minds are influential, often coloring our perceptions with brushes dipped in the past's dark ink.

Understanding the Power of Place

Places are not just physical locations; they are tapestries woven with stories of their past, soaked in emotions that persist through time. A place reputed for hauntings carries with it a heavy cloak of expectation. When we hear tragedies or untimely deaths associated with a location, our minds are primed to expect abnormal occurrences. This expectation sets a stage where ordinary shadows assume sinister forms, and every sound hints at spectral presences. Recognizing how deeply these narratives can influence our perception is crucial before claiming a paranormal experience.

The Role of Psychological Factors

Psychological factors play a significant role in shaping what we perceive as paranormal. *Our brains are pattern-seeking missiles*, always trying to make sense of random information, especially in high-stress situations like exploring an allegedly haunted house.

Fear heightens our senses, making us more susceptible to mistaking mundane occurrences—like the house settling or branches brushing against a window—as supernatural events.

Rational Approaches to Haunted Experiences

Developing rational approaches involves peeling back layers of lore to scrutinize the logical explanations beneath. Suppose we understand the psychological underpinnings and historical contexts that seed ghostly expectations. In that case, we equip ourselves with a critical mindset necessary for any seasoned ghost hunter.

This mindset not only aids in debunking less plausible claims but also sharpens our ability to discern genuinely unexplainable phenomena from those born of fear and folklore.

Approaching haunted places without preconceived notions lets us objectively analyze each creak and whisper. By understanding that human emotions can taint our experiences, we learn to filter out the noise created by our expectations. This chapter aims to arm you with tools to challenge you and understand why we see what we see in these shadowed halls.

Towards a New Paradigm in Ghost Hunting

As we journey through haunted sites armed with knowledge and critical insight, our experiences become more prosperous and more grounded in reality. We transform from spectators of spooky tales into astute observers of human psychology and environmental influence. This shift is not just about debunking myths but enhancing our understanding of human perception and its incredible impact on our interpretation of the unknown.

So, as you turn each page, remember: **the journey into haunted places is as much about exploring the mysteries of human consciousness as it is about investigating unexplained phenomena.** Let's step beyond the veil of folklore, guided by curiosity and armed with knowledge, ready to face whatever lies in the shadows—not with fear, but with a desire to understand the true nature of these haunted spaces.

History and Lore: Setting the Stage for Ghostly Expectations

The history and stories attached to a location often lay a rich foundation for expectations of paranormal happenings. A castle with a history of tragic deaths or an old house where unresolved mysteries linger naturally sets the stage for eerie sensations. These stories, passed down through generations or sensationalized by the media, prime visitors to expect ghostly encounters even before they step foot on the property.

Consider this: when you walk into a movie theater knowing you're about to watch a thriller, your senses are heightened; every shadow and sound might make you jump. Similarly, when you enter a place known for its haunted history, your mind is already preparing for a spooky experience.

The lore of a place does more than tell a story; it creates an atmosphere. This atmosphere plays a crucial role in shaping visitors' experiences. The psychological impact of a place's lore can be profound, influencing what you might see or hear and how you interpret benign happenings as supernatural.

For example, a sudden chill in an old room can be easily explained by drafts, but in haunted lore, it becomes a spectral touch. This is how powerful a location's backstory can be—it transforms ordinary occurrences into moments of paranormal intrigue.

A simple analogy to understand this would be how a filter changes the appearance of a photograph. The lore acts as a filter through which the reality of a place is perceived, coloring every creak and whisper with the hue of the supernatural.

Haunted places are often steeped in stories that set expectations for ghostly encounters, influencing what visitors experience.

Psychological Influences on Paranormal Perceptions

Our minds are potent interpreters, often influenced by subtle cues that shape our perception of reality. Psychological factors, such as suggestion, expectation, and emotional contagion, can significantly alter what we perceive in haunted locations.

Suggestion plays a pivotal role. When a guide tells you a room is haunted, it plants an idea in your mind. This suggestion makes you more alert to anomalies that you might otherwise dismiss.

Expectation builds on this; as you start to anticipate paranormal events, your brain is on high alert for any signs that align with this expectation.

Being in a group can amplify these sensations. Emotional contagion, or the spread of feelings from one person to another, can make anxiety or fear more intense. If one person jumps at a sound, others are likely to react similarly, escalating a group's overall fear response.

The power of the mind to transform sensory data based on expectations cannot be underestimated. It filters and interprets inputs based on what it expects, often blurring the lines between the ordinary and the paranormal.

Have you ever wondered how much of a ghostly encounter is shaped by our minds?

Rationalizing Paranormal Experiences with Historical Context

To approach haunted locations critically, it's crucial to understand how their histories and stories influence our perceptions. By analyzing the backstory, we can begin to demystify experiences that seem paranormal.

First, consider the source of the haunting story. Many tales grow more elaborate over time, gaining layers of details that may have little basis. Researching the actual history of a location can often provide more straightforward, more rational explanations for supposed hauntings.

Next, critically evaluate personal experiences against this backdrop. If you hear footsteps in an old house, could they be caused by settling structures or loose floorboards? Understanding a location's physical characteristics can often explain seemingly mysterious phenomena logically.

A helpful step-by-step approach involves documenting experiences and matching them against the lore and physical facts of the location. This method helps distinguish between what might genuinely be inexplicable and what can be explained through logic and understanding of the environment.

By understanding the influence of a location's lore and critically evaluating experiences within that context, we can separate fact from fiction and approach haunted places with a rational, analytical mindset. This understanding bridges the gap between fearful expectation and logical analysis, empowering us to explore these mysteries with a critical eye.

Wrapping Up Our Exploration

As we delve into the shadows of haunted places, we uncover stories of the past and reflections of our inner psyche. The journey through this chapter has shown us how deeply **historical narratives and psychological factors** are intertwined with our perceptions of paranormal phenomena. By recognizing the impact of a location's lore, we can better understand how we expect to be shaped, often setting the stage for ghostly experiences.

Our exploration has emphasized the **importance of a critical mindset**. When faced with tales of hauntings, it's crucial to dissect these stories with a rational approach. This does not strip away the mystery or allure of haunted places; rather, it enhances our understanding and appreciation by grounding our experiences in reality. Through this lens, every creak and whisper in an old house is not just a signal from the beyond but also a call to unravel the complex tapestry of history and human emotion woven into its walls.

Developing methods to **rationalize paranormal experiences** based on a location's backstory equips us with tools to navigate and demystify the unknown. This approach fosters a healthier relationship with our fears and curiosities, allowing us to confront ghostly tales with skepticism and respect for their narrative roots.

Reflecting on these insights, we are reminded of the power of stories and how they can transform ordinary places into realms of extraordinary experiences. As we move forward, let us carry the torch of inquiry and skepticism, illuminating the paths through haunted halls with the light of reason and understanding.

Let this chapter serve as a cornerstone for budding ghost hunters and curious minds, guiding them through the fog of myth and misconception with clarity and purpose. Embrace these lessons as you continue your journey, equipped with tools to challenge paranormal claims and more profound wisdom about the human condition and our eternal fascination with the unknown.

Chapter 3: Ghost Hunting Gadgets: Tools or Toys?

Can Science Illuminate the Shadows of the Paranormal?

In the dimly lit corridors of the old Lancaster mansion, where whispers of the past seemed almost tangible, Thomas walked with an EMF detector in hand. His eyes scanned the device's fluctuating numbers, reflecting a mix of skepticism and intrigue. The air was thick with the musty scent of decayed wood and long-forgotten secrets. As he wandered through the creaking halls, his mind grappled with memories of his father—a staunch scientist who had always dismissed ghost stories as mere distractions from logical reasoning.

The house moaned under its weight as if groaning at Thomas's attempts to uncover its supposed mysteries. He paused by a large, dust-covered portrait that seemed to watch him with stern disapproval. "Dad always said to look for logical explanations first," he mutters, recalling how his father would explain natural phenomena with unwavering rationality.

Thomas' thoughts were interrupted by a sudden spike in his EMF detector. His heart quickened—was this the proof he needed? Or just another electrical fault, as mundane as those his father used to diagnose and fix in their old home? The cold draft that danced along his spine suggested more than faulty wiring; it whispered doubts and fears about what he might find.

Outside, the wind wrestled with the ancient trees surrounding the mansion. Their branches tapped against windows like desperate fingers seeking attention. Inside, Thomas felt a chill that wasn't entirely because of the draft. He remembered his father's words: "Science is about questioning, not confirming biases." Was he discovering a hidden truth or becoming entangled in his hopes?

As he prepared to leave the room, a floorboard beneath him groaned loudly, echoing through the silent house like a cry for attention. Then, Thomas realized how deeply intertwined fear and curiosity could become when one ventured into unknown territories without fully understanding their tools.

Is our search for ghosts merely a reflection of our desire to find something beyond what science can explain?

Are Your Tools Unveiling Ghosts or Just Glitches?

When embarking on a journey into the unknown realms of ghost hunting, the allure of high-tech gadgets can be irresistible.

Enthusiasts and professionals alike often equip themselves with an array of devices, each promising closer encounters with the paranormal. Yet, how frequently do we question whether these tools reveal spirits or amplify our spectral fantasies?

In the fascinating world of paranormal investigation, the line between reality and misinterpretation is as thin as a wisp of mist.

The equipment, ranging from EMF detectors to infrared cameras, looks impressive and feels essential. However, without a proper understanding of what these gadgets truly measure and how they work, even the most seasoned ghost hunter can be led astray by readings that are less about ghosts and more about mundane environmental factors.

Understanding Your Toolkit

The journey starts with a clear-eyed look at the **standard tools** used in ghost hunting. Initially designed for entirely different purposes—such as identifying electrical faults or recording temperature changes—these devices have been repurposed in the hunt for the paranormal. It's crucial to ask: Are we interpreting their signals correctly?

The Science Behind the Scare

Embracing a scientific approach means acknowledging that **not all flickers are ghostly**. EMF detectors, for instance, can spike because of faulty wiring or other commonplace electrical issues rather than spectral presences. Learning about these potential pitfalls enriches our understanding and sharpens our investigative skills.

From Assumption, to Evidence

In this exploration, we must also consider how to *apply scientific principles* effectively. This involves setting up controlled environments, conducting repeat experiments, and keeping meticulous records—all practices that elevate ghost hunting from mere thrill-seeking to something approaching a rigorous science.

This chapter invites you on a reflective journey to demystify the tools of the trade. Through anecdotes from seasoned investigators and insights from experts in fields as diverse as physics and psychology, we'll peel back layers of assumption to reveal more precise truths.

The goal here isn't to debunk or belittle the passion for paranormal investigation but to refine and define it with a sharper empirical edge. By fostering a deeper understanding of our tools and tendencies, we empower ourselves as ghost hunters and as discerning seekers of truth in all its forms.

Join me in this thrilling exploration. It's an enlightening venture that promises to make us better investigators and thoughtful world observers. Whether you're a skeptic or a believer, there's undeniable value in questioning and learning—after all, isn't the search for truth at the very heart of every ghost story?

Exploring Common Tools Used in Ghost Hunting

Ghost hunting relies heavily on various gadgets, often seen as a bridge between the mysterious spiritual world and our own. One such device frequently used is the **EMF detector**. Originally designed to identify electrical faults and ensure safety in wiring and power systems, EMF detectors are now a staple in ghost hunting kits. The assumption here is that spirits can manipulate or disturb the electromagnetic field.

Imagine you're a carpenter, using a hammer to drive nails into wood and check the firmness of the ground. Just as a hammer isn't designed for geological testing, EMF detectors weren't crafted with ghost detection in mind. This mismatch can lead to misinterpretations, attributing ordinary electromagnetic fluctuations to paranormal activity.

The infrared thermometer is another tool often found in the ghost hunter's arsenal. Professionals use these devices to detect heat leaks or monitor industrial equipment, and they pick up temperature variations. In ghost hunting, sudden cold spots are often interpreted as a sign of spectral presence. However, understanding the natural causes of temperature shifts, such as drafts or air conditioning units, is necessary to claim a ghostly cause.

Using these tools outside their intended purpose can be likened to using a stethoscope to listen to the murmur of a distant ocean. While creative, this isn't different from what the tool is made for, and it may lead to inaccurate or meaningful interpretations.

Thermal cameras also find their way into paranormal investigations. Initially designed for building inspections, military operations, and other practical applications, these cameras can detect humans and animals in complete darkness based on body heat. However, variations in materials or the cooling effects of breezes can also create patterns that are easily mistaken for supernatural phenomena.

The key takeaway is that understanding these tools' original purpose and limitations is crucial in ghost hunting. Misuse can lead to false positives, transforming simple electrical interferences or natural temperature variations into ghostly encounters.

Analyzing the Limitations and Misinterpretations

When delving into ghost hunting, it's essential to question the reliability of the equipment used. Like using a household thermometer to measure the temperature of a volcano, employing devices outside their intended scope can yield misleading results.

This misapplication often stems from a lack of understanding of the scientific principles underlying these gadgets.

EMF detectors, for instance, are sensitive to a range of electromagnetic emissions, not just those purportedly given off by ghosts. Everything from your home's wiring to appliances can influence an EMF reading. Without critically evaluating the surroundings, one might hastily attribute a spike in EMF to paranormal activity.

Interpretation plays a significant role. A sudden drop in temperature captured by an **infrared thermometer** might set a ghost hunter's heart racing. However, without considering other environmental factors, this could be a draft passing through an old window, not a spectral visitor.

The allure of **thermal cameras** in ghost hunting also needs scrutiny. These cameras can indeed reveal figures not visible to the naked eye. Still, they can also be fooled by the mundane—an animal moving in the brush or the residual heat from a recently operated machine.

Reflect on this: When we're eager to confirm our beliefs, might we see what we wish to see rather than what's truly there? Could our desires cloud our interpretations?

How often might a simple explanation suffice if we will consider it?

Applying Scientific Principles in Ghost Hunting

Bringing scientific scrutiny into ghost hunting doesn't strip away the thrill; rather, it enhances the credibility of the findings. Just as a detective gathers evidence without jumping to conclusions, a ghost hunter must use tools with an understanding of their scientific basis.

Consider the EMF **detector**. Knowing its sensitivity to electromagnetic sources allows a ghost hunter to rule out false positives. Documenting all electromagnetic sources in an area before concluding a paranormal origin ensures a more credible investigation.

Using an infrared **thermometer** demands a similar approach. By accounting for all potential natural sources of temperature change, a ghost hunter can more confidently assert that any remaining anomalies might have a less mundane explanation.

This scientific approach can be likened to sifting flour in baking. Just as one removes lumps to ensure a smooth batter, removing logical explanations for anomalies ensures that what remains might be out of the ordinary.

By embracing the scientific roots of their equipment, ghost hunters can transform their investigations from mere curiosity into disciplined inquiries. This commitment to rigor bolsters their credibility and enriches the field, paving the way for more definitive encounters with the unknown.

These learning objectives guide us in using tools responsibly, interpreting data critically, and applying rigorous scientific methods to enhance the integrity of paranormal investigations.

Throughout this exploration of ghost-hunting tools, we've unearthed the **origins** and functions of devices commonly used in paranormal investigations. Tools like EMF detectors, initially designed to detect electrical issues, have been repurposed in the quest to identify the supernatural. However, the excitement and mystery of ghost hunting often lead to a **misinterpretation** of what these gadgets detect.

Reflecting on these insights, it's imperative to approach ghost hunting with a **skeptical and scientific mindset**. Remember, the allure of connecting with the unknown should not cloud our judgment or skew the interpretation of data. As enthusiasts and investigators, our responsibility is to question and validate findings through rigorous scientific methods. This approach enhances the credibility of our investigations and sharpens our understanding of the natural world.

Let's consider an anecdote about a seasoned investigator who used an EMF detector in an old mansion reputed to be haunted. Initially, the readings were off the charts, leading many to believe in a paranormal presence. However, upon closer inspection and more structured scientific analysis, it was discovered that the high readings were because of outdated electrical wiring rather than spectral inhabitants. This story is a potent reminder that **not all that buzzes is ghostly**.

By embracing this disciplined approach, you are not just chasing shadows but contributing to a field that thrives on precision and factual accuracy. This journey of discovery does not merely aim to debunk myths but to uncover deeper truths that lie at the fringes of our understanding.

As we continue this exploration in the subsequent chapters, remember that each tool has its story, and each anomaly is a lesson waiting to be learned. With an open mind and a scientific toolkit, the journey through the world of paranormal investigation promises not just thrills but profound insights into the boundaries between science and folklore.

Let us move forward with curiosity and rigor, always ready to question, always eager to learn. In doing so, we honor both the seen and the unseen realms of our experience, navigating through shadows with the lantern of science and skepticism.

Chapter 4: The Critical Thinker's Guide to Paranormal Phenomena

Can Curiosity Outshine Fear?

In the dimly lit corner of an old library, nestled between towering shelves laden with dusty tomes and forgotten manuscripts, sat Eleanor. Her eyes danced over the pages of a heavy, leather-bound book on paranormal investigations. The musty air mingled with the scent of aged paper, forming a cocoon around her as she absorbed words steeped in mystery and skepticism.

Outside, the sun dipped below the horizon, casting long shadows that played across the room like spectral fingers. Eleanor's heart quickened with each gust of wind that moaned through the cracked windows as if whispering secrets from ages past. She was alone in this pursuit tonight, driven by a need to understand rather than fear what lay beyond the veil of death.

Memories of her grandmother's tales fluttered through her mind like delicate moths. The old woman had spoken of spirits with both reverence and caution—a balance that Eleanor now sought to find through critical thinking. She remembered how her grandmother's voice would soften when recounting her encounters with the ghostly apparitions in their family home. Those stories ignited Eleanor's curiosity and sowed doubt about what lurked in those unexplained shadows.

As she turned another page, a sudden chill swept through the room, interrupting her thoughts. The candle flickered violently, as if protesting against an unseen force. Eleanor's breath caught in her throat; it was moments like these when fear clawed at her reason.

Yet she steadied herself, recalling the principles of logical inquiry she had just read about. Was there a draft she had not noticed?

Could the candles dance be nothing more than a reaction to a natural cause?

Pulling her shawl tighter around her shoulders, Eleanor rose and paced along the rows of books. Her fingers brushed against spines embossed with golden letters, each touch grounding her back to reality—a reality where every shadow and every sound had an explanation waiting to be uncovered.

She paused near a window overlooking the library's ancient oak tree, whose branches scratched against the glass like skeletal hands tapping for attention. In this moment, between curiosity and rationality, Eleanor felt most alive here—most connected to her grandmother's world and her pursuit of truth.

Could understanding these forces truly allow us to master our fears?

Are You Truly Seeing Ghosts, or Is It Just Your Imagination?

Welcome to a profound journey through the maze of paranormal phenomena where the line between reality and illusion often blurs.

In our quest to unravel the mysteries that linger in the shadows, we must arm ourselves with one indispensable tool: **critical thinking**.

This chapter refines your analytical skills, enhancing your ability to separate fact from fiction when confronted with claims of the supernatural.

At its core, ghost hunting is an exhilarating blend of curiosity and adventure. However, it is also rife with unverified claims and ambiguous evidence. The thrill of encountering the unknown can sometimes lead us astray, causing us to accept eerie explanations without solid proof. Here, we emphasize the significance of **tangible, logical evidence** in validating paranormal claims. By demanding clear evidence, we uphold a standard that protects us from deception and helps maintain the integrity of the paranormal investigation.

Developing critical thinking skills is more than necessary—it's a transformative process that shifts how we perceive and interact with the unseen world. By cultivating these skills, we empower ourselves to debunk pseudoscientific explanations that often cloud the truth. This chapter will guide you through understanding various cognitive biases and logical fallacies that can distort our judgment. Recognizing these pitfalls is the first step toward objectively analyzing paranormal events.

Transitioning from a fear-driven to a curiosity-driven approach to ghost hunting does not diminish the thrill; rather, it enriches our experiences by grounding them in reality. Fear often leads to hasty conclusions and blurred perceptions. Curiosity fosters patience and attention to detail—traits essential for any seasoned investigator who wishes to uncover the truth behind ghostly apparitions.

Throughout this chapter, expect personal anecdotes that highlight these principles at work. These stories serve as practical examples and connect us through shared experiences of mystery and discovery. They remind us that behind every shadow and whispered tale, a story is waiting to be understood through the lens of critical inquiry.

This exploration is not just about debunking myths; it's about opening new doors of understanding. It invites you to view ghost hunting not merely as chasing after shadows but as an opportunity to explore human perception, history, and even physics.

As we embark on this insightful journey together, remember: The goal is not simply to disprove but to discover. Transforming fear into fascination and confusion into clarity requires nothing less than courage—the courage to question, think critically, and, most importantly, remain open-minded in our spectral pursuits.

Emphasizing the Importance of Tangible Evidence

When approaching the enigmatic world of paranormal phenomena, the first step is always to seek tangible, logical evidence. This is fundamental because physical evidence can be observed, tested, and verified, unlike abstract notions or hearsay. For instance, when investigating a haunted house, rather than relying solely on stories of past residents or blurred photographs, a critical thinker would look for concrete signs like unexplained electromagnetic field (EMF) readings that are consistent and reproducible under similar conditions.

Imagine you're a detective in a mystery novel. Your goal isn't just to listen to the town gossip but to find clues that give you undeniable proof of what's happening. In paranormal investigation, this means favoring sensor readings and digital recordings that can be analyzed scientifically over personal testimonials that cannot be replicated.

Focusing on tangible evidence helps eliminate biases that often cloud human judgment. While personal experiences are exciting and emotionally resonant, they are subjective and can be influenced by many external factors, such as one's beliefs or the environment.

Objective evidence is independent of individual perceptions.

This emphasis on physical evidence is not about debunking all paranormal claims but establishing credibility and reliability in investigations. Doing so makes it possible to discern paranormal phenomena from mere misconceptions or fabrications.

Tangible, logical evidence is the cornerstone of valid paranormal investigations.

Cultivating Critical Thinking to Debunk Pseudoscience

Critical thinking is an indispensable skill in the toolbox of anyone keen to delve into paranormal investigations. It involves absorbing information and actively questioning it, breaking it down, and analyzing its components. This skill set is crucial when confronting pseudoscientific explanations often accompanying paranormal claims.

To cultivate such skills, start by understanding the scientific method, which is based on observation, hypothesis, experimentation, and conclusion. When a paranormal claim is made, applying this method involves observing it, forming a hypothesis about its nature, conducting experiments to test this hypothesis, and drawing conclusions from the results.

Use rhetorical questions to challenge assumptions. For instance, if a light flickers in an old house and someone claims it's because of paranormal activity, ask: "What other explanations could there be?

Could it be an electrical issue or simply the age of the wiring?"

Incorporating analogies can also aid understanding. Think of critical thinking as the immune system of the mind, defending against the viruses of misinformation and irrational beliefs. Just as our immune system needs exposure to pathogens to develop strength, our minds need exposure to diverse viewpoints and challenging questions to build robust critical thinking.

Practicing these skills leads to a more thorough scrutiny of evidence, helping to separate scientifically plausible explanations from unfounded ones. This process clarifies the nature of the paranormal claim and enriches the investigator's understanding of the natural world.

Is your mind equipped to dissect truth from embellishment in the tales of the unknown?

Transitioning from Fear to Curiosity in Paranormal Investigation

The shift from a fear-driven to a curiosity-driven approach in ghost hunting can transform the experience from apprehension to exploration and learning. This transition is crucial for personal comfort and the investigation's integrity.

Fear can cloud judgment, leading to biased interpretations of ordinary events as paranormal. For example, a sudden chill might be perceived as a ghostly presence rather than a draft. In contrast, approaching the same situation with curiosity drives one to seek all explanations, fostering a more comprehensive understanding of the event.

Imagine a child in a dark room. If they are scared, every shadow might seem like a monster. But if they are curious, they might explore further and discover that what seemed like monsters are just ordinary objects casting shadows.

The Critical Thinking Framework

The framework introduced here, tailored for dissecting paranormal claims, comprises several critical components that foster analytical skills and promote a skeptical yet open-minded approach.

Identifying the Claim

The first step is to neutrally understand the paranormal claim, capturing its essence without bias. This involves listening carefully and documenting the claim thoroughly, ensuring no preconceived notions color the initial understanding.

Evaluating the Evidence

Next, the importance of tangible, physical evidence over anecdotal or hearsay evidence is emphasized. Criteria for assessing the robustness and relevance of presented data are provided, encouraging a focus on evidence that can be seen, measured, and verified.

Applying Occam's Razor

This component encourages identifying the simplest explanation that accounts for all observed phenomena. It discourages leaping on supernatural explanations without exhaustive exploration of natural ones, promoting logical simplicity and clarity.

Identifying Logical Fallacies

Arming with the knowledge to recognize common reasoning errors helps avoid misleading or distorted conclusions. Understanding these fallacies protects the investigator from jumping to conclusions unsupported by evidence.

Constructing Rational Arguments

The last part of the framework guides the formulation of premises based on evidence and conclusions grounded in logic. This step-by-step guide helps construct coherent and rational arguments against pseudoscientific explanations.

These components interact dynamically, each crucial role in building a solid investigation. For instance, identifying logical fallacies can prevent improper evidence evaluation, and applying Occam's Razor can simplify the entire process by eliminating overly complex theories unsupported by solid evidence.

These learning objectives guide us from seeking solid evidence to sharpening our analytical abilities to shifting our approach from fear to curiosity, forming a comprehensive strategy for paranormal investigation.

As we wrap up this exploration of paranormal phenomena, it's essential to remember the power and necessity of critical thinking.

This approach is not just about debunking myths or dismissing stories as mere fantasies; it's about engaging with the unknown rationally and respectfully. The journey through tangible, logical evidence allows us to separate fact from fiction, ensuring our curiosity is grounded and ignited.

Critical thinking is paramount, serving as the backbone of effective paranormal investigation. It equips us with the tools to question and analyze, pushing us beyond mere spectators of mysterious tales into active investigators of our world. By demanding solid evidence and logical reasoning, we empower ourselves to confront the unknown without fear, transforming our approach from apprehension to intrigue and discovery.

One of the most profound changes we can make is to shift from a **fear-driven** to a **curiosity-driven** approach to exploring ghostly phenomena. This transformation turns the eerie noises in the dark from reasons to fear into puzzles to solve and challenges to understand. This transformation is not just about changing how we hunt ghosts; it's about reshaping how we view the unknown parts of our world.

Reflecting on our own experiences and those of others, we've seen how easily unverified claims or sensational stories can sway the mind. By fostering a mindset that prioritizes evidence and logical thinking, we're not just better ghost hunters—we're more discerning observers of unexplained phenomena. This skill is invaluable, allowing us to navigate life with a healthy skepticism and a keen eye for truth.

By embracing these principles, we step into a broader world rich with mysteries waiting to be understood rather than feared.

Let's carry this curiosity and rigorous inquiry mindset as we continue our journey. Let the unknown not deter us but drive us to learn more, understand better, and explore further with open minds and critical eyes.

Chapter 5: Decoding the Past: Historical Insights into Hauntings

Can History Unveil the Mysteries of the Haunted?

On a fantastic autumn evening, as the sun dipped below the horizon, casting long shadows over the old town of Eldridge, Edward Mills stepped out onto the cobblestone streets. His breath formed small clouds before him as he walked briskly toward the ancient library at the heart of town. The grand stone structure library was rumored to have been built on grounds where once soldiers had fallen during forgotten battles. Whispers in town spoke of haunting echoes and shadows that moved with no bearer.

Edward, a historian by profession and a skeptic by nature, carried a heavy leather-bound notebook filled with facts and folklore about Eldridge. He had lived here all his life, but only now did the stories of ghosts begin to gnaw at his curiosity. Each step he took resonated against the stones like a drumbeat calling spirits from their rest.

Inside, under the warm glow of an oil lamp, he laid out maps and texts across a large oak table that groaned under their weight. His eyes scanned over documents yellowed with age; they whispered tales of wars, treaties signed and broken, lives lived and lost. Edward felt a chill run down his spine—not from any spectral presence, but from the cold draft sneaking through ancient windows.

As he delved deeper into his research, Marjorie, an elderly librarian with knowledge as vast as her smile was wide, approached him. "Finding what you're looking for?" she asks in her gentle voice that seemed to smooth out even the crumpled pages before him.

"Not yet," Edward replies without looking up. "I'm trying to find any unusual deaths or events right here where this library stands."

Marjorie chuckles softly and adjusted her glasses. "Oh dear," she says as she pulled up a chair beside him. "This place has more history than most know what to do with."

They talked for hours; Marjorie recounted stories handed down through generations, while Edward noted every detail meticulously.

He searched for logical explanations to combat tales of hauntings, believing that history held the keys to understanding these modern-day myths. With her wealth of knowledge, Marjorie became an invaluable ally in Edward's quest for the historical truths behind the hauntings.

As midnight approached and they prepared to leave, Edward stood by one of the large windows overlooking the town square where the fog rolled in like silent waves on an invisible shore.

Could understanding truly dispel fear? Or does our search for explanations merely lead us deeper into mysteries we can never fully unravel?

Can History Unveil the Secrets of Haunted Places?

When we hear tales of haunted houses or ghostly encounters, our curiosity is piqued by the supernatural element and the historical tapestry that frames these stories. This chapter delves into how a thorough understanding of historical contexts can dramatically alter our perception of paranormal claims. Imagine walking through an old, creaky house; knowing its history not only adds depth to the experience but might also demystify some of its eerie reputation.

The foundation of our exploration rests on the premise that **historical context is crucial** when interpreting reports of hauntings. Just as detectives look for motives in a crime scene, ghost hunters can benefit significantly from investigating the past events associated with a location. This approach satisfies historical curiosity and is a pivotal tool in distinguishing between myths and plausible explanations for paranormal phenomena.

Why History Matters in Paranormal Investigation?

Consider this: many haunted locations have backgrounds steeped in tragedy or conflict. Knowing whether a building was the site of a historical battle provides insights that might explain reports of paranormal activities. It's not just about proving or disproving ghostly encounters; it's about understanding why people believe what they do. This knowledge can be empowering and enlightening, transforming a spooky tale into a fascinating historical narrative.

The Role of Research in Unveiling Truths

Researching historical events related to alleged hauntings is more than an academic exercise; it's a detective mission that can offer explanations where myths have previously dominated. Like a detective piecing together clues from a crime scene, we can uncover forgotten stories that shed light on present-day ghost stories. This process helps us challenge widely held beliefs with factual data, potentially debunking myths or providing context that explains why certain spirits are said to linger.

Challenging Folklore with Facts

In confronting folklore, we arm ourselves with facts to engage in informed skepticism. This doesn't mean dismissing every ghost story as false; instead, it involves scrutinizing the stories through the lens of historical evidence. By doing so, we honor both the tales and the truths of the past, allowing us to separate fact from fiction respectfully and thoughtfully. This approach not only respects the beliefs of others but also enriches our understanding of the past and present.

This chapter aims to equip you with tools for better understanding haunted places and inspire you to look beyond the surface stories.

The insights gained here encourage a deeper appreciation for history's role in shaping our perceptions of the paranormal. As we move forward, remember that every shadow and whisper from an old wall may not be a specter from beyond but echoes of a vivid past calling out to be understood and acknowledged.

Appreciating Historical Context

The past whispers to us through the walls of old buildings and the tales of those who once lived there. Understanding the historical context of these places is like reading the user manual before trying to operate a complex piece of machinery. Without this knowledge, the actual function—or, in our case, the true story—remains obscured by assumptions and myths.

Imagine you're hearing footsteps in an old house at night. Now, knowing that the house once served as a busy tavern in the 18th century, where weary travelers would stop to rest, suddenly the creaks and whispers might seem less like spirits and more like echoes of a bustling past life. This shift in perception underscores how historical context can transform our understanding of seemingly paranormal events.

Historical records are treasure maps, leading us to the stories behind the legends fueling ghost tales. When a house with a reputation for being haunted turns out to be a former hospital or a battlefield, these facts can explain many of the mysterious occurrences people report. Shadows and sounds often have more to do with history than hauntings.

By peeling back the layers of history, we often find that what we thought were supernatural events are interactions with the remnants of human lives and activities imprinted on a place. This is not to diminish the allure of a good ghost story but to enrich it with the depth of real human experiences.

Embracing the Importance of Historical Context in Interpreting Paranormal Claims

Conducting Historical Research

To investigate any haunted locale, one must first become a history detective. Where do you start? Public records, old newspapers, and local folklore are good starting points. Each piece of evidence can shed light on the mysterious occurrences people report.

Imagine you're investigating an old schoolhouse reputed to be haunted. Through old newspapers, you discover it was once used as an emergency hospital during a flu epidemic. Suddenly, reports of moaning sounds take on a new meaning. They are not evidence of the paranormal but of the place's poignant past.

Engaging with local historians or library archives can unearth forgotten events that once took place on the property. This research might reveal that the land was once a settlement with a tumultuous history, which can explain many of the disturbances attributed to ghosts.

But how does one sift through all this information? A helpful approach is to create a timeline of the property's history, noting any events that could contribute to its haunted reputation. This systematic process clarifies the origins of ghost stories and connects you more profoundly with the local heritage.

This research method can often dispel myths and illuminate the facts, turning eerie tales into enriching historical narratives. So, when you hear a floorboard creak or see a shadow flit by in a supposedly haunted house, ask yourself: What historical events occurred here?

Could understanding the past be the key to unlocking the mysteries of today?

Challenging Folklore with Facts

Once the historical groundwork is laid, the next step is to challenge the existing folklore with the facts uncovered. This is where our investigation can shift from exploring to explaining, from what is told to what is known.

Consider a house rumored to be haunted by the ghost of a white woman. Historical research might reveal that the house was built on an old textile mill site where many women worked under harsh conditions. The "woman in white" could be a symbolic remnant of those workers, misinterpreted as a ghostly presence.

This rational approach involves comparing ghost stories with historical data. In doing so, we often find that the supernatural elements of these stories align closely with human history, not paranormal activity. By presenting these findings, we can shift the narrative from one of fear to one of understanding and respect for the past.

Using analogy here is like turning on a light in a dark room. The shadows that once seemed menacing are revealed to be ordinary objects. Similarly, the ghosts that haunt our tales often turn out to be echoes of genuine historical tragedies or every day past events.

By challenging folklore with factual historical data, we transform ghost stories from spooky tales into meaningful connections with our past.

Bringing It All Together

Understanding a location's historical backdrop is essential to interpreting reports of hauntings. Thorough research into the site's history can often rationally explain these ghostly claims.

By challenging the existing folklore with uncovered facts, we move from mystery to understanding, enriching our appreciation of history and the present. This approach demystifies supposed hauntings and deepens our connection to the places we live and visit.

Understanding a location's historical backdrop offers invaluable insights into its alleged hauntings. It is fascinating how much the past can illuminate the present wildly when unraveling paranormal claims mysteries. We've taken significant strides toward rationalizing ghostly reports by appreciating the historical context, conducting thorough research, and challenging folklore with factual data.

Historical context is crucial when interpreting these eerie occurrences. Remember, every site has its story, steeped in years, decades, or even centuries of human experience. These stories can shed light on why certain places feel haunted. For instance, knowing that a building was once a hospital during a historic battle helps explain reports of ghost sightings or mysterious sounds—what might initially seem supernatural could be echoes of a turbulent past.

Conducting research is not just about digging through archives or scrolling through old newspapers—it's about piecing together a place's life. Each document, photograph, and artifact adds a layer to our understanding, helping us see beyond the myths. This process satisfies curiosity and equips us with the facts needed to debunk or validate claims of hauntings.

Perhaps the most exciting part is challenging folklore with factual historical data. It involves a dynamic interplay between myth and reality, where we learn to separate fact from fiction. This doesn't mean dismissing people's experiences outright but approaching them discerningly. It's about being detectives in a world teeming with mysteries, where our most incredible tool is our ability to question and analyze.

As we move forward in our journey of paranormal investigation, let's carry with us the lessons learned from this chapter. Let's remain curious, skeptical, and, above all, respectful of the past as we seek to understand the mysteries of the present. Our exploration is far from over, but we become more adept at distinguishing shadows from specters and folklore from fact with each step.

Keep this spirit of inquiry alive as you explore the unknown. Armed with historical knowledge and a critical mind, you are well-equipped to tackle any ghostly challenge that comes your way.

Remember, in the world of paranormal investigation, understanding the past may be your key to unlocking the secrets of the present. So, keep questioning, keep researching, and most importantly, enjoy every moment of discovery.

Chapter 6: Technological Tools: Beyond the Lens and Microphone

Can Technology Truly Capture the Ghosts of the Past?

Eleanor stood still in the middle of the old library, her fingers brushing against the dusty spines of forgotten books. The air was thick with the musty scent of aging paper and wood, a testament to decades of silent stories echoing through the dimly lit halls. She clutched her digital audio recorder tightly, a lifeline in the overwhelming quiet that enveloped her.

Her mind wandered to the technology she wielded — cameras, recorders, electromagnetic sensors — designed to pierce the veil between known and unknown realms. She remembered how, during her last visit, a whisper had broken through the static of her headphones. This faint murmur seemed almost like a sigh from centuries past. These moments fueled her pursuit, yet doubt lingered like an uninvited shadow at each step.

Outside, a branch tapped against a windowpane as if trying to get her attention. Eleanor jumped slightly, pulled back into reality by nature's nudge. She chuckled at herself; years in this field and still startled by an autumn leaf's playful dance against the glass. With its creaking floors and whispers, this place held more than just academic interest for Eleanor; it was personal. Her great-grandfather had been a caretaker here, his tales of ghostly encounters woven into their family fabric like golden threads.

As she set up her camera to document any unusual occurrences tonight, Eleanor thought about all those who dismissed her efforts as mere chases after the wind. Her peers' skepticism often echoed louder in her ears than any spectral voice captured on tape. Yet something deep within urged her forward — was it hope or merely a desire not to let go?

She paused momentarily and glanced around at the towering bookshelves standing guard like sentinels over forgotten knowledge. What secrets did they hold? Could her devices capture proof of what lurked beyond human senses, or were they merely extending the reach of age-old human hopes against oblivion?

Eleanor knew interpreting what these devices picked up was as crucial as capturing anything. Misinterpretation could lead one down false paths, as misleading as any phantom maze.

Tonight might yield nothing more than usual — some unexplained noises, perhaps a temperature drop near the history section — but each investigation brought Eleanor closer to whatever truth lay hidden within these walls.

As she settled down on an ancient oak chair with her equipment ready for the night's vigil, she couldn't help but wonder: Are we genuinely hunting ghosts, or are we just chasing echoes of our past fears and desires?

Unraveling the Digital Ghosts: A Guide to Tech-Savvy Paranormal Investigations

Embracing Technology in the Quest for the Paranormal

The quest to understand the paranormal has often been shadowed by skepticism and disbelief. In this era of advanced technology, we have tools that can transform mere tales of the unknown into verifiable scientific data. This chapter delves into how technology, when wielded correctly, can become a crucial ally in substantiating or debunking paranormal claims. It's not just about capturing a fleeting shadow or an unexplained whisper; it's about understanding the capabilities and limitations of technological tools in paranormal research.

The Double-Edged Sword of Technological Evidence

While technology offers new vistas in paranormal investigation, it also brings challenges that can lead to misinterpretation of data. A sound recorded on an EVP (Electronic Voice Phenomenon) device might seem like a clear-cut case of paranormal activity. Still, without proper analysis, it could well be radio interference or background noise misidentified as something otherworldly. As investigators, we must approach each piece of evidence critically, ensuring that what we present as potential proof withstands rigorous scrutiny.

Mastering Your Tools: From Novice to Expert

The journey from a novice using a digital recorder to an expert analyzing spectral audio is filled with learning and adaptation. In this chapter, you will learn how to use different recording devices during field investigations effectively. This involves understanding how they work, finding the optimal configurations, and following established guidelines to ensure accurate data collection. Knowing your equipment inside out enhances the credibility of the data collected and boosts your confidence as an investigator.

Analytical Skills: The Heart of Data Interpretation

Beyond collection lies the critical phase of **data interpretation**.

This involves distinguishing between false positives—commonplace explanations mistaken for paranormal—and genuine anomalies. Analytical skills come to the forefront as you learn to dissect audio clips, video recordings, and other forms of digital data to uncover the truth hidden within them.

Objectivity: The Keystone of Paranormal Investigation

Maintaining objectivity is one of the most challenging aspects when faced with seemingly inexplicable phenomena. Excitement and personal beliefs can cloud judgment, leading to biased conclusions. This section underscores the importance of approaching each investigation with a neutral mindset, focusing on facts rather than interpretations influenced by personal biases.

Learning from Mistakes: Anecdotes from the Field

This chapter incorporates anecdotes from seasoned investigators to highlight common pitfalls in using technology and celebrate these mistakes as valuable learning opportunities. Each story reminds us that errors are steppingstones to becoming more proficient in handling and interpreting technological data in ghost hunting.

By understanding the power and limitations of modern technology in ghost hunting, we better equip ourselves to face the unknown.

This journey requires patience, critical thinking, and an unwavering commitment to uncovering the truth—wherever it may lead. As we move forward in this chapter, let's embrace these tools with curiosity and skepticism, refining our methods so that our findings can confidently stand up to scientific inquiry and public scrutiny.

Understanding the Dual Nature of Technological Tools in Paranormal Research

The advancement of technology has significantly empowered paranormal investigators, equipping them with tools that can detect and record phenomena beyond the capabilities of the human senses. These instruments are essential for capturing often elusive evidence, from high-definition cameras to sensitive audio recorders. However, their efficiency doesn't guarantee accuracy; these tools can also mislead, capturing data that, without scrutiny, may be misinterpreted as paranormal.

Imagine a typical scenario where an investigator uses a thermal camera during an investigation. The camera picks up a heat signature that appears humanoid. It's easy to conclude that this is a spectral presence. However, this is where the potential pitfall lies. Without a deep understanding of how thermal cameras work and what else could cause such readings—such as the residual heat from a radiator or a living being recently occupying that space—an investigator might falsely identify it as paranormal.

This highlights investigators' need to use technology and comprehend its workings deeply. Knowing the limitations and strengths of each piece of equipment can save one from falling into the trap of false positives. For instance, understanding that specific camera lenses can create lens flares that might look like orbs is crucial. This knowledge ensures that conclusions are based on solid evidence rather than equipment artifacts.

Audio recording devices are invaluable for capturing sounds whispering from beyond. Yet, these devices can equally pick up interference from radio frequencies or background noise, which can be misconstrued as voices. The critical task is distinguishing between genuinely anomalous sounds and those mundane but masked by the recorder's sensitivity.

Understanding the capabilities and limitations of technological tools is fundamental to paranormal research.

Mastering the Usage of Recording Devices

To capture reliable data in paranormal investigations, one must master the intricacies of using recording devices. These devices, when used correctly, can provide irrefutable evidence of paranormal activity, but their misuse can as quickly generate false positives. Learning to operate these tools precisely is akin to learning to play a musical instrument; both require understanding, practice, and a keen ear for subtleties.

Start by selecting the right equipment. High-quality digital audio recorders with adjustable sensitivity settings are preferable. These allow the change of recording thresholds to minimize background noise while capturing faint, unexplained noises. Similarly, video cameras should have night vision or infrared capability to record in low-light conditions where paranormal activity is often reported.

The positioning of equipment is equally crucial. Audio recorders, such as buzzing electrical devices or busy streets, should be protected from potential interference. Cameras should have a clear field of view, with attention paid to eliminating reflections and other visual distortions that could be mistaken for paranormal phenomena.

Reflect on this: when setting up cameras and microphones, the environment is as much a part of your toolkit as the devices themselves. Understanding your location's acoustic and lighting properties can dramatically affect the quality of the data captured.

Reviewing and adjusting the equipment settings throughout an investigation can prevent hours of recording unusable data. It's important to periodically check the equipment to ensure it functions as expected and adjust to environmental changes.

Applying Analytical Skills to Data Interpretation

Once data is collected, the actual work begins. Applying analytical skills to interpret this data objectively separates seasoned investigators from amateurs. It's not just about collecting evidence; it's about understanding what it represents.

Firstly, the data should be reviewed in its raw form. Look for any anomalies and note them for further analysis. This initial step is crucial as it sets the stage for a deeper investigation into each piece of evidence.

The next step involves comparing the noted anomalies against known causes. For instance, if a voice is captured on an audio recorder, check for sources of interference, like radio frequencies or overlapping conversations from nearby locations. This is where a solid understanding of the equipment and its vulnerabilities comes into play.

Imagine you are a chef tasting a dish to discern the different ingredients. Similarly, dissecting audio or visual data layers to identify what is truly out of the ordinary requires a discerning mind. This process often involves using software to enhance the audio or visual data and isolate the components of interest.

Finally, corroborate your findings. If multiple pieces of equipment capture the same anomaly under different settings, the likelihood of it being a genuine paranormal event increases. This cross-verification is a cornerstone of credible paranormal investigation.

By understanding technology's potential and pitfalls, mastering its use, and applying critical analytical skills, investigators can more reliably distinguish the paranormal from the normal.

Mastering the art of using recording devices in paranormal research is akin to becoming a skilled detective. The journey begins with **diligently selecting** the most suitable tools for the job. Whether digital voice recorders, video cameras, or EMF detectors, each device has specific strengths and limitations. Understanding these tools thoroughly by studying manuals and conducting test recordings in various settings lays a solid foundation for credible investigations.

Strategic placement and meticulous change in these devices during fieldwork must be addressed. Ensuring that cameras and recorders are positioned to capture a comprehensive field of view or focus on areas with reported activities significantly enhances the chances of documenting genuine phenomena. Adjusting settings like resolution or audio sensitivity helps capture more explicit, reliable data.

The real challenge, however, lies in the **objective analysis** of the collected data. This requires a keen eye and an unyielding commitment to scientific rigor. Critical steps include analyzing recordings with specialized software, looking for inconsistencies or anomalies in audio and visual feeds, and correlating these with environmental conditions. Here, one must remain vigilant, guarding against the allure of jumping to paranormal conclusions without robust evidence.

Documenting every detail of the investigation process also plays a crucial role. This not only aids in maintaining the integrity of the data but also provides valuable insights for future investigations. Every recorded data point, observed anomaly or environmental condition should be meticulously noted.

Lastly, the field of paranormal research is ever-strengthened. Staying updated with the latest technological advancements and continuously refining recording techniques based on personal experiences and broader community insights is essential. This dynamic approach ensures that your investigative methods remain current and effective.

Through this structured yet flexible approach, enthusiasts can transform their investigations from ghost hunts to severe inquiries into the paranormal. By embracing technology with a critical mind and a thorough understanding of its capabilities and limits, you stand the best chance of uncovering the truth behind the mysterious and the unexplained. Remember, in paranormal research, **every detail and finding contributes** to a more extensive understanding of the unseen world.

Chapter 7: Witness to the Weird: Conducting Effective Interviews

Can the Truth of a Haunting Be Captured in a Single Interview?

Eleanor sat by the window of the small café, nestled in the heart of Savannah's historic district, where whispers of the past seemed to seep through the cobblestone streets. Her gaze drifted across the street where an old colonial house stood, its windows like hollow eyes and its doors slightly ajar, as if beckoning with secrets. Today, she was to meet Mr. Aldridge, a man who claimed his ancestral home was haunted.

A cup of black coffee sat before her, untouched, steaming gently into the cool autumn air. Eleanor's mind wandered to her previous encounters with eyewitnesses — each a delicate dance of words and silences, where too much eagerness could color the truth as effectively as disbelief.

Mr. Aldridge arrived, his steps echoing on the wooden floorboards of the café. He was an elderly man with sharp eyes that seemed to hold decades of untold stories. As he sat down opposite her, Eleanor noted how his hands trembled slightly — not with age, but perhaps with what he had experienced.

"Thank you for meeting me," Eleanor began softly, setting her recorder between them but keeping her eyes fixed on his face rather than her equipment. "I understand this might be difficult for you."

Mr. Aldridge nodded, his voice barely above a whisper as he started recounting nights filled with inexplicable shadows and whispers that threaded through his home like cold drafts from unseen cracks.

As he spoke, Eleanor listened intently, not just to what he said but how he said it — each pause laden with memories or perhaps fear. She knew that effective interviewing required more than just gathering facts;

it demanded empathy and patience to allow the story to unfold at its own pace without direction or interruption.

Outside, a gust of wind swept through the street, rattling against windowpanes and sending leaves skittering across sidewalks in frenzied spirals. The sound seemed almost like sighs from another time stirring around them. Mr. Aldridge described a chilling encounter when he felt someone watching him from an empty room.

Eleanor noticed how other patrons glanced over occasionally—drawn not by eavesdropping but by something in Mr. Aldridge's tone that broadcast urgency mixed with desperation—a plea for understanding, if not belief.

As their interview ended and Mr. Aldridge stood to leave—looking somehow lighter yet infinitely tired—Eleanor reflected on what she had learned, not just about ghostly phenomena but human nature's capacity for resilience in the face of unexplainable events.

She remained seated after he left, pondering her notes, filled with raw data that still needed sifting for clarity and truth among shadows of doubt and fear.

Can we ever truly discern reality from illusion when dealing with tales as old and deep as those haunted souls tell?

Can You Handle the Truth?

Unlocking the mysteries behind paranormal phenomena hinges significantly on the quality of information gathered from those who claim to have witnessed such events. As we delve deeper into the art of ghost hunting, your role in **conducting interesting interviews** with eyewitnesses becomes paramount. Your interviews are more than mere conversations; they are structured opportunities to gather invaluable insights without contaminating the testimony with preconceived notions or biases. This chapter aims to equip you with the skills to extract precise, unbiased narratives from those who've experienced the unexplainable.

The Art of Listening

When investigating paranormal claims, the ability to listen actively and without judgment is critical. Every detail in an eyewitness account can provide clues about the witness's experience.

Fostering an environment where interviewees feel heard and respected increases the likelihood of obtaining comprehensive, undistorted information. We will explore techniques emphasizing neutrality in interviewing—asking open-ended questions and letting the witness lead the conversation—which helps minimize any influence over their responses.

Building Trust

Trust is the cornerstone of any meaningful interview. Witnesses of paranormal phenomena often hesitate to share their experiences for fear of disbelief or ridicule. Creating a rapport and showing genuine interest in their stories puts them at ease and opens avenues for more detailed and honest accounts. This chapter discusses strategies to establish trust quickly and effectively, ensuring that witnesses feel safe and valued throughout the interview.

Discerning Fact from Fiction

One of the most challenging aspects of paranormal investigation is distinguishing credible testimonies from those skewed by external influences or personal biases. It requires a keen understanding of human psychology and a systematic approach to questioning. We'll delve into recognizing common patterns that might show embellishment or misinterpretation and learn how to probe deeper into such areas to clarify ambiguities tactfully.

Practical Application

The skills discussed here aren't just theoretical; they're designed for immediate application in real-world scenarios. Whether you're a novice ghost hunter or looking to refine your interviewing techniques, this chapter offers step-by-step guidance that can be implemented right away. From setting up the interview environment to choosing your questions wisely, each element plays a vital role in shaping the outcome of your investigations. By integrating these practices into your investigative toolkit, you enhance your efficiency as an investigator and contribute substantially to the broader field of paranormal research. Effective interviewing does more than gather facts; it builds a foundation for understanding what lies beyond our current knowledge.

By integrating these practices into your investigative toolkit, you enhance your efficiency as an investigator and contribute substantially to the broader field of paranormal research. Effective interviewing does more than gather facts; it builds a foundation for understanding what lies beyond our current knowledge. Your role in this mission is crucial, and your contributions will help shape the future of paranormal research.

As we progress through this chapter, remember that each interview is a unique encounter with someone's reality regarding phenomena many have yet to comprehend fully. Approaching these interviews with humility, curiosity, and respect can open doors to realms previously thought unreachable by conventional methods. Let's embark on this journey together, mastering the art of extracting truth amidst tales of the unknown.

Learning Objective One: Neutral and Effective Interview Techniques

Mastering the art of interviewing is as crucial as a detective piecing together clues at a crime scene when diving into a paranormal investigation. Each conversation with an eyewitness is a unique opportunity to gather untainted and insightful information that could prove pivotal in understanding the supernatural occurrence.

Consider yourself as a sculptor. Just as a sculptor uses tools to shape a formless block of marble into a defined figure, an interviewer uses questions to shape the scattered thoughts of an eyewitness into a coherent account. The key here is to use the right tools — questions that are open-ended and free of bias. These allow the witnesses to express their experiences fully without being swayed by the interviewer's preconceptions. As an interviewer, your role is not to impose your views but to facilitate the witness's narrative, ensuring their story is told in their own words.

Effective interviewing hinges on neutrality. This means refraining from leading questions that suggest a desired answer. For instance, instead of asking, "Did you feel scared when you saw the ghost?" a neutral question would be, "How did you feel during your experience?" This subtle shift encourages a witness to provide a genuine and personal response.

Another important aspect is maintaining a calm and non-judgmental demeanor. Witnesses are often wary of sharing their experiences for fear of disbelief or ridicule. Establishing a rapport where they feel safe and understood is paramount. It involves active listening, nodding, and occasionally paraphrasing their words to show that you are engaged and value their account.

Effective interviewing is not just about gathering facts; it's about understanding the human experience behind the paranormal event.

It's like reading a book in which each page offers a deeper insight into the story rather than merely collecting scattered notes.

The essence of effective interviewing in ghost hunting is neutrality, enabling the witness to narrate their story without influence.

Learning Objective Two: Fostering Open and Honest Accounts

The truth is often shrouded in layers of mystery and emotion in the paranormal realm. To peel back these layers, an interviewer must create an environment that encourages open and honest communication.

Let's consider the importance of the setting. A comfortable and familiar environment can significantly affect a witness's willingness to open up. Whether it's a quiet corner of a café or their living room, the setting should reassure the witness, making them feel secure enough to share their experiences freely.

Questions are the bridge to hidden truths. Crafting open-ended and empathetic questions not only garners detailed responses but also shows respect for the witness's experience. For example, "What happened next?" allows the witness to control the narrative, providing details that might be missed with a simple yes or no question.

Reflective listening is a powerful tool in this process. It involves echoing what the witness has said to make them feel heard and prompt them to continue. This technique validates their experience and deepens the conversation, revealing more nuanced information.

Using silence effectively can also encourage a witness to elaborate on their experiences. In our fast-paced world, silence can be uncomfortable. However, an interview can be valuable for the witness to organize their thoughts and share more profound insights.

Imagine each interview as a dance in which the interviewer and the witness move together in rhythm, uncovering truths step by step. This delicate dance requires patience, empathy, and a genuine interest in understanding the witness's experience.

Does how we listen and respond to a witness alter the depth of truth they will share?

Effective Interview Framework

The Preparation Phase

The first phase of the Effective Interview Framework focuses on preparation. Before meeting with a witness, conducting thorough background research is crucial. This includes reviewing any existing evidence, previous testimonies, and the historical context of the paranormal event. Such preparation ensures that the interviewer is well-informed and can ask relevant questions that probe deeper into the witness's account.

The Engagement Phase

Building rapport is the cornerstone of the engagement phase. Here, the interviewer connects with the witness, creating a comfortable atmosphere. Simple gestures like maintaining eye contact or offering a warm, reassuring smile can make all the difference. This phase sets the stage for open communication, making the witness feel respected and understood.

The Questioning Phase

The questioning phase is where the core of the interview takes place. A blend of open-ended questions and more direct queries allows the interviewer to guide the conversation effectively while allowing the witness to express themselves. This balance is critical in a comprehensive picture of the event, imposing no biases.

The Critical Listening Phase

Active and critical listening during this phase allows the interviewer to absorb the witness's account fully. This involves hearing their words and noticing the nuances of their expressions and emotions. Such detailed attention helps assess the credibility of the testimony and identify any inconsistencies.

Verification Phase

The ultimate phase involves verifying the facts, and claims made during the interview. This could include cross-referencing with other testimonies, checking historical records, or consulting with experts. This step is vital in ensuring that the information collected is reliable and can be used effectively in the investigation.

The Effective Interview Framework is a dynamic process that adapts to the flow of each conversation. It ensures that every interview is conducted with a structured approach, yet remains flexible enough to accommodate the unique aspects of each witness's story.

By integrating these phases effectively, we can ensure that the interviews conducted during paranormal investigations are both credible and insightful, aligning with the goals of neutrality, openness, and honesty.

Mastering the Art of the Interview: A Pathway to Unveiling Paranormal Truths

Effective interviewing is a cornerstone of paranormal investigation, providing vital insights into eyewitness accounts of unexplained phenomena. The techniques discussed in this chapter ensure that every interview you conduct captures the essence of the eyewitness's experience and does so with integrity and accuracy.

By establishing a comfortable environment and building trust, we encourage open and honest communication, which is crucial for gathering untainted data.

Active listening and asking **open-ended questions** are fundamental to this process. These skills allow the interviewer to delve deeper into the witness's account without leading or biasing the testimony. Remember, the goal is to let the eyewitness tell their story in their own words, providing as much detail as possible. This approach respects the witness's perspective and enriches the quality of the information collected.

Recording the interview with consent ensures no detail is lost and provides a resource for future analysis. It's important to take detailed notes as well, capturing not just the facts but also the emotional context of the experience, which can be incredibly telling.

Evaluating the credibility of the testimony is one of the most challenging aspects of the interview process. It requires a balance of skepticism and open-mindedness. By comparing the eyewitness account with other testimonies and evidence, you can begin to discern patterns and inconsistencies that will aid in forming a more complete picture of the paranormal event.

Finally, expressing gratitude to the eyewitness for their participation underscores the respectful and professional approach necessary for effective paranormal investigation. It reassures the eyewitness that their experience is valued and taken seriously, which can be profoundly validating for them.

By following these steps, you equip yourself with a powerful toolset to conduct thorough and respectful interviews that can significantly enhance the investigation of paranormal claims. Each interview adds to your understanding of individual incidents and contributes to the broader field of paranormal research, helping to peel back the layers of mystery surrounding these intriguing phenomena.

Remember, every story holds a piece of the puzzle. It's our job to listen carefully, analyze thoughtfully, and piece together the truth with as much clarity and objectivity as we can muster.

Chapter 8: Unveiling Mysteries with Science: The Real Ghost Busters

Can Science Unravel the Mystery of the Haunted Manor?

In the dim twilight, James wandered through the creaking halls of the old manor, his steps echoing in the vast emptiness. The house, aged by time and shrouded in tales of ghostly apparitions, stood as a monument to unexplained phenomena. As a scientist devoted to logic and empirical evidence, James had been drawn here by stories that chilled the bones of even the most skeptical locals.

The air was thick with dust and history. He could feel the weight of countless stories pressing down upon him, each corner whispering secrets of ages past. The manor's reputation as haunted was not just folklore but an invitation—a challenge—to his scientific mind.

Earlier that day, James had spoken with Mrs. Aldridge, an elderly neighbor who insisted that at night, one could hear faint whispers and see fleeting shadows in these halls. Her voice had trembled, not with fear but with certainty. "It's them," she'd say softly, "the ones who never left." Such certainty from a rational neighbor had pushed James to consider what forces could cause such convictions.

As he moved from room to room equipped with various instruments—EMF meters, thermal cameras—he recalled his days as a student when he first learned how infrasound or mold spores could trigger feelings traditionally associated with hauntings. These memories fueled his quest for a logical explanation for what others deemed supernatural.

Each measurement and sample collected spoke to him not of ghosts but of natural anomalies yet to be fully understood in this context.

Was it possible that what people experienced was merely a reaction to something imperceptible yet perfectly natural?

He paused by a large window overlooking the estate's overgrown garden, letting the cool breeze brush against his face. The moon cast long shadows across the lawn, creating patterns that danced silently in the night. A sudden chill caused him to shiver, not from cold. Still, from a realization—perhaps there was more interplay between our senses and our surroundings than he had accounted for.

Lost in thought about how human perception could twist reality into spectral experiences, he almost missed the soft thud from upstairs—a sound out of place in this still night—which pulled him back sharply from his reverie.

Could scientific analysis strip away all layers of mystery woven into the human experience over centuries? Or did some elements remain defiantly inexplicable?

Are Ghosts Real or Just a Trick of the Mind?

Few topics capture the imagination in the realm of the unexplained, quite like ghostly encounters. But what if I told you that many of these spine-tingling tales could be unraveled by science? This exploration does not diminish the mystery but enriches our understanding, empowering us with knowledge and reducing unfounded fears. This chapter delves into how scientific methods can debunk and demystify paranormal claims, turning eerie experiences into explainable events.

The power of scientific **investigation** lies in its systematic approach to understanding phenomena. By applying this rigor to cases of alleged hauntings, we uncover environmental and physical explanations that often go unnoticed. For instance, did you know that carbon monoxide leaks can induce hallucinations that some interpret as supernatural? Or can infrasound—sound waves below the range of human hearing—create feelings of unease or even terror? It's insights like these that transform our approach from fear to curiosity.

As we progress, we'll explore specific techniques and tools that anyone can use to investigate suspicious events scientifically. From thermal imaging cameras to electromagnetic field (EMF) detectors, you'll learn how each tool helps paint a clearer picture of what might initially seem inexplicable. This hands-on knowledge equips us to tackle ghostly mysteries and enhances our general critical thinking skills.

We'll examine case studies where logical deductions have clarified seemingly paranormal occurrences. These real-life examples provide exciting evidence of how a scientific lens can shift our interpretation of events from supernatural to natural. Each case study is a testament to the power of inquiry and rational thought in confronting the unknown.

This journey through science is not just about debunking myths; it's about embracing a more informed perspective on the world.

Understanding what causes these mysterious experiences reduces unnecessary fear and opens us up to genuine awe at the natural world's complexities.

Let's arm ourselves with knowledge and turn from fearful witnesses into skilled investigators, ready to unveil the truth behind every shadow and whisper. After all, isn't understanding reality's true nature the most incredible adventure? Join me as we step into the role of real-life Ghostbusters, using science as our guide through the shadows.

Apply Scientific Methods to Investigate and Explain Reported Paranormal Phenomena

When faced with the unexplained, jumping to supernatural conclusions is easy. However, applying scientific methods provides a structured way to demystify these phenomena. By employing objective observations, controlled experiments, and critical thinking, we can shift from speculation to understanding.

Imagine you're a detective, but instead of solving crimes, you're unraveling the mysteries of a haunted house. Like a detective, a paranormal investigator uses tools—not magnifying glasses and fingerprint kits, but EMF meters and infrared cameras. This analogy helps us grasp how systematic the process is, focusing on gathering evidence before concluding.

Scientific investigation begins with meticulous observation. Documenting the conditions under which paranormal activities are reported is crucial. Noting witnesses' time, environmental conditions, and psychological state can offer initial insights that guide further inquiry.

The next step involves forming hypotheses. If a door slams shut, could it be because of air pressure changes rather than a spectral presence? Developing testable ideas about these occurrences strips away layers of mystery and opens the door to empirical testing.

Experimentation follows, where hypotheses are tested. This might involve replicating the conditions reported during the paranormal event to see if the outcome is the same. Through this process, we can identify natural explanations for phenomena that initially seemed inexplicable.

The key to demystifying paranormal claims is rigorous adherence to scientific inquiry, ensuring our conclusions are based on evidence rather than conjecture.

Explore Environmental and Physical Factors that Can Lead to Misinterpreted Experiences

Often, what is perceived as paranormal is merely a misinterpretation of environmental cues. For instance, low-frequency sounds, known as infrasound, can create discomfort and even hallucinations, yet are undetectable to the human ear.

Consider the role of carbon monoxide in reputed haunted houses.

This odorless gas can cause severe health problems, including hallucinations and feelings of dread. Detecting and measuring such factors can often provide simple explanations for seemingly mysterious experiences.

Old houses are prone to creating creepy sounds. As the wood expands or contracts, it can mimic footsteps in the attic or whispers in the walls. Electrical issues can cause flickering lights or electronic disturbances, common elements in ghost stories.

Why do we often feel a chill down our spine in specific environments? Drafts and poor insulation might be the culprits, not ghostly presences. Investigating these factors explains the phenomena and improves living conditions by addressing the issues.

Visual illusions can also trick us. Dim lighting and the human brain's tendency to recognize faces and figures—pareidolia—can turn shadows into specters.

Could understanding our surroundings be the key to unlocking the mysteries behind many haunted tales?

Use Logical Deductions to Solve Cases Traditionally Deemed Supernatural

Logical thinking is the most reliable tool in the investigator's kit. Just as Sherlock Holmes used deduction to solve complex cases, we can apply these principles to unravel supposed paranormal mysteries.

Consider a scenario where multiple witnesses report seeing apparitions in an old theater. Instead of concluding that the theater is haunted, an investigator might analyze the sightings' commonalities, perhaps discovering reflective surfaces or peculiar lighting as the cause.

Scientific Method Framework for Paranormal Investigation

This framework is a structured approach to understanding and investigating paranormal phenomena scientifically. Let's break down each component:

Observation

The cornerstone of scientific inquiry is observation. Here, we gather detailed, unbiased data about the reported paranormal activity. This step is crucial, as it forms the foundation for building hypotheses. Investigators document everything without assuming a supernatural cause.

Hypothesis Formulation

Next, we develop plausible, natural explanations for the observations. These hypotheses should be clear and testable and aim to explain phenomena using known scientific principles.

Experimentation

We then test these hypotheses through experiments. This may involve recreating the conditions of the paranormal event under controlled settings to see if the outcome can be replicated without invoking supernatural explanations.

Data Analysis

After experiments, the collected data are analyzed rigorously to see if they support the hypotheses. This step is vital for determining whether the explanations hold or need refinement.

Critical Evaluation

This stage involves scrutinizing the results and considering alternative explanations. It's about being open to adjusting or even discarding hypotheses based on the evidence.

Iteration

Science is never static. This last step emphasizes the need to refine methods and hypotheses continually based on new insights and outcomes from previous investigations.

This dynamic model shows how components interact and depend on each other, creating a robust method for investigating paranormal claims. The framework not only aids in debunking unfounded claims but also deepens our understanding of the phenomena by grounding them in reality.

By applying scientific methods, exploring environmental influences, and using logical deductions, we can solve many mysteries attributed to the paranormal.

As we've navigated the enthralling journey of applying scientific rigor to paranormal investigations, the essence of this chapter crystallizes into a transparent, actionable process that can transform any curious observer into a proficient investigator. This method enhances understanding and empowers us to approach mysteries with confidence and skepticism. Let's reflect on the profound impact of integrating scientific methods in demystifying paranormal phenomena and how you can implement these strategies effectively.

The Spectral Sleuth's Methodology

Define the research question or hypothesis. Begin by pinpointing exactly what you aim to uncover or prove. For instance, question whether a so-called haunted site has explainable, natural causes behind its eerie reputation.

Conduct a literature review. Knowledge is power. Delve into existing research to build a firm foundation for your investigation, drawing on the available scientific literature.

Design the investigation. Tailor your research plan to adhere to scientific principles. This might involve setting up control environments or choosing reliable measurement tools.

Collect data systematically. Accuracy is key. Gather your data methodically to maintain consistency and reliability, ensuring your conclusions will be well-founded.

Analyze the data using statistical methods. Crunch the numbers to see whether they support or debunk your original hypothesis.

This step is crucial in validating your findings.

Consider alternative explanations. Keep an open mind. Explore all possible natural explanations for observed phenomena, challenging your assumptions and strengthening your conclusions.

Consult with experts. Sometimes, two (or more) heads are better than one. Engaging with experts can provide new insights or confirm your deductions.

Document and present findings. Transparency builds trust. Record your methodology, analysis, and conclusions clearly and concisely, making them accessible for review or further investigation.

Seek peer review and feedback. Collaboration enhances credibility. Share your findings with peers to refine your approach and validate your results.

Repeat and refine the investigation. The pursuit of knowledge is never-ending. Revisit your investigation with modifications to solidify the reliability and accuracy of your conclusions.

Each step is designed as a task and a steppingstone toward greater understanding and proficiency in paranormal investigation. By adopting this systematic approach, you engage in a dynamic learning, analyzing, and developing process, which is essential in any scientific endeavor.

This structured approach does more than solve mysteries—it educates and empowers. It encourages critical thinking, nurtures curiosity, and, most importantly, replaces fear of the unknown with knowledge and understanding. As you continue on your journey through this guide, remember that each mystery unraveled is not just an answer but a step towards becoming a more insightful, discerning observer of the world.

Let this process be your compass in the vast sea of the unknown, guiding you to clearer shores where the line between myth and reality is seen and understood.

Embrace this journey of discovery, and let the thrill of solving the unsolvable enrich your pursuit of truth in the shadows of the paranormal.

Chapter 9: From Fear to Fascination: Educating the Paranormal Enthusiast

When Knowledge Lights the Shadows

In the heart of an old New England town, where the leaves painted the ground in a mosaic of autumn hues, Eleanor stood before the ancient library that had whispered tales to her since childhood. Its walls, cloaked in ivy, held secrets of a time when candlelight flickered through its windows and shadows danced on its stone floors. Armed with curiosity sharpened by years as a historian, Eleanor was here to explore and confront her own shadows.

Inside, the air was thick with the scent of aged paper and whispers of the past. She walked past rows of books, their spines cracked and worn like wise old men leaning into each other, sharing secrets.

Her fingers brushed against the leather-bound spines, feeling their histories etch into her skin. Today was different; she sought answers about the local hauntings that had colored her childhood with both dread and wonder.

Eleanor paused by a window overlooking the graveyard next door.

The sun cast long shadows over tombstones, standing guard like silent sentinels. It was here among these graves that ghost stories were born—tales that had frightened her as a child but now sparked only a thirst for truth. She remembered nights huddled under covers as the wind howled like wandering spirits outside her window.

Turning back to an old oak table, she spread out her notes—articles, maps, diary entries from townsfolk long passed. Each piece was a puzzle waiting to find its place in history's vast tapestry. Eleanor's skepticism mingled with academic rigor as she delved into eyewitness accounts of spectral figures and unexplained lights. Could understanding these phenomena through research strip them of their power to frighten? Was fear merely ignorance disguised?

A floorboard creaked behind her—a reminder that even libraries breathe and settle into their foundations. She smiled faintly at this thought; it was another mystery explained away by simple facts.

How often do we let our fears grow unchecked in the shadowy corners of our ignorance?

Embrace the Unknown: Transforming Fear into Curiosity

Understanding the paranormal does not begin in haunted mansions or fog-laden graveyards; it starts within the confines of our minds, where fear often establishes deep roots. Our natural reaction to the unknown can stifle our curiosity or propel us towards enlightenment. This chapter delves into how knowledge is a powerful tool to transform fear into a profound fascination with the mysteries surrounding us.

The Power of Knowledge Against Fear

Fear is a primal response, hard-wired into our beings, serving as both protector and captor. Regarding the paranormal, fear often stems from misconceptions and the portrayal of the unknown in popular media as something to be feared rather than understood.

However, by shifting our approach from fear-driven to knowledge-driven exploration, we empower ourselves to face these mysteries with confidence and curiosity. This transformation is not just about accumulating facts but also about changing how we perceive the unexplained.

Cultivating Curiosity about Rational Inquiry

Curiosity is the antidote to fear. It compels us to ask questions, seek answers, and challenge preconceived notions. By fostering a **curiosity and rational inquiry** mindset, we equip ourselves with the tools to systematically explore paranormal claims. This mindset goes beyond surface-level knowledge and aims to understand phenomena on a deeper level by questioning not only "what" and "how," but also "why."

Knowledge Sharing: Debunking Myths

One of the most powerful outcomes of gaining knowledge is the ability to share it. Misinformation about the paranormal creates a breeding ground for fear. By disseminating what we learn, we educate others and contribute to a more significant cultural shift towards more skeptical and rational perspectives on paranormal claims. This shift has profound implications not only for individual understanding but also for how society at large interacts with and interprets the paranormal.

The upcoming sections will explore these themes, providing philosophical insights and practical advice on transforming your approach to paranormal investigation. You will learn how replacing fear with curiosity opens new possibilities for understanding and interacting with the world.

This chapter offers a friendly hand to guide you through often misunderstood territory. Personal anecdotes highlight common fears and misconceptions about hauntings and supernatural events.

By embracing this new perspective, you enrich your experiences and encourage those around you to view paranormal claims through a lens of informed skepticism.

The journey from fear to fascination is not just about changing beliefs; it's about fostering an attitude that values evidence and critical thinking, paving the way for more enlightened discussions about what lies beyond our current understanding. Join me as we embark on this transformative journey together, exploring how knowledge can turn eerie whispers in the dark into voices that we understand and perhaps even appreciate.

Transforming Fear into Knowledge

Imagine standing in a dark room, hearing every creak and whisper, your heart racing with every shadow. Often a primal reaction to the unknown, this fear is a common starting point for many encountering the paranormal. But what if we could arm ourselves with knowledge instead of fear?

In paranormal exploration, fear typically stems from a lack of understanding. The unknown terrifies us. However, by transitioning to a knowledge-driven approach, we equip ourselves with the tools to demystify the shadows. Learning about the scientific methods to investigate and explain paranormal phenomena can transform fear into a rational curiosity.

Consider the analogy of learning to swim. Initially, the water seems daunting, deep, and dangerous. But with lessons and understanding, fear slowly dissipates, replaced by confidence and enjoyment. Similarly, educating oneself about the paranormal changes the nature of the experience from horror to fascination.

Each step in gaining knowledge about the paranormal not just educates but empowers. It shifts the narrative from being a victim of fear to a curious investigator, sparking a new level of engagement and fascination.

Knowledge replaces fear and empowers exploration, giving you the confidence to delve into the unknown.

Curiosity and Rational Inquiry

Curiosity is a powerful catalyst for learning. In the paranormal context, fostering curiosity involves challenging the initial fear-based reactions and encouraging a more inquiry-based approach.

Why do we hear certain sounds? What causes the sensation of being watched? By asking questions, we start on a path of rational exploration, stimulating our intellect and eagerness to learn.

A fundamental aspect of nurturing this mindset is understanding the scientific method and how it applies to paranormal investigation. This involves observing phenomena, forming hypotheses, conducting experiments, and drawing conclusions.

These steps encourage a systematic approach to what often seems like chaotic and unexplainable experiences.

Think of a detective in a mystery novel. The thrill is not just finding out who the culprit is but piecing together the small, seemingly unrelated details. In paranormal investigation, each detail and each question leads you closer to understanding the true nature of the experience.

Developing a curiosity-driven approach requires patience and persistence. It's about continuously questioning and being open to discovering alternative explanations. This mindset demystifies the paranormal and enriches the investigator's experience.

How can we transform our innate fear of the unknown into a powerful drive for discovery?

Sharing Knowledge to Debunk Myths

Education plays a pivotal role in demystifying the paranormal. By sharing knowledge, we empower ourselves and influence the broader community's perceptions of supernatural phenomena.

Debunking myths is not just about proving what's not real; it's about understanding the natural explanations behind seemingly paranormal occurrences.

For instance, consider the impact of infrasound—sound waves below the range of human hearing. Infrasound can create feelings of unease or even terror, which some might attribute to supernatural causes. Educating others about such scientific explanations helps reduce fear and promotes a more rational approach to the paranormal.

Using analogies can help explain complex ideas. Just as a magician's tricks become less mysterious once you know how they are performed, understanding the science behind paranormal experiences can demystify them. This knowledge can transform fear into fascination and skepticism into inquiry.

Sharing this knowledge can take many forms, from writing articles and books to hosting workshops and talks. Each act of sharing helps dispel myths and encourage a more informed, rational approach to the paranormal.

By transforming fear into knowledge, fostering curiosity, and sharing our findings, we empower ourselves and others to approach the paranormal with confidence and scientific insight.

Embracing the unknown with confidence and curiosity is not just a shift in perspective; it's a transformative journey that reshapes our encounters with the paranormal. When knowledge replaces fear, each shadow and unexplained noise becomes a potential discovery rather than a source of terror. This profound transformation from fear to fascination is liberating and profoundly empowering.

Knowledge is a powerful tool that demystifies the myths surrounding paranormal phenomena by understanding the how and why behind seemingly inexplicable events. Enthusiasts are equipped to approach their explorations with a grounded and rational mindset. This does not diminish the thrill of the hunt; rather, it enhances the experience by rooting it in reality and making it accessible to everyone.

Fostering a mindset of curiosity is essential. It encourages continuous learning and questioning, which is vital in challenging the stigmas associated with paranormal investigation. This curiosity-driven approach promotes a more thorough and systematic examination of claims, leading to more reliable and substantive conclusions. By adopting this approach, enthusiasts enrich their understanding and contribute to a broader cultural awareness of the paranormal.

The sharing of knowledge plays a crucial role in debunking widespread myths. By educating others, enthusiasts help spread a more rational and less sensationalized view of paranormal activity.

This knowledge dissemination helps reduce fear and encourages a more inclusive conversation about what it means to explore the unknown.

The journey from fear to knowledge involves changing how we perceive the unexplained and how we engage with the world.

Armed with facts and a keen eye for detail, what once seemed daunting becomes intriguing. This shift benefits those directly involved in paranormal exploration—it enriches our collective understanding and fosters a society that values evidence over superstition.

As we move forward, let us confidently carry this ethos into every dark corner and shadowed hallway. Let the flashlight of knowledge guide us through the mysteries of the paranormal, illuminating truths waiting just beyond the reach of our former fears.

Chapter 10: The Rational Hunter: Science Over Sensationalism

Can Science Illuminate the Shadows of the Supernatural?

The late afternoon sun filtered through the dusty windows of an old library in a forgotten corner of Edinburgh, casting long shadows that seemed almost sentient, creeping slowly across the worn wooden floorboards. James stood among rows of ancient books, a middle-aged man with skeptical eyes and a demeanor that hinted at countless nights spent chasing phantoms that science had yet to explain. His fingers brushed against the spines as if he could absorb their knowledge through touch.

Today was different. Today wasn't about proving or disproving myths but understanding them. In his mind, he replayed his last encounter at a reputedly haunted mansion on the city's outskirts. In this place, whispers from the past seemed as natural as the chill that settled into your bones in its presence.

James paused, pulling out a volume so old its title had faded into obscurity. He opened it, and a musty smell wafted up to meet him, blending with the aroma of aging paper—a scent that spoke of secrets and stories untold. As he flipped through pages yellowed by time, his thoughts wandered back to last night's investigation. The equipment had malfunctioned, but there was something else—unaccountable cold spots and soft sighs in the dark that no gadget could detect.

A few tourists entered the library, and their voices suddenly entered his reverie. They laughed lightly among themselves, oblivious to the deeper search unfolding. James watched them for a moment before returning to his book; their dismissal of ghost stories as mere entertainment echoed society's broader skepticism—a skepticism he often shared but occasionally questioned.

The clock struck an hour closer to evening, pulling James back from his thoughts. He needed tangible evidence to bridge the gap between legend and fact. Could truths be laid out in these tales, waiting for someone patient enough to uncover them? Could science truly illuminate what has been dismissed as mere shadows?

As he prepared to leave with notes tucked under his arm and uncertainty lodged firmly in his chest—his quest continued: Is there room for ghosts in scientific inquiry, or are they just figments born from our love for mystery?

Why Ghost Hunting Should Be More Science, Less Spectacle

The allure of the unknown has often led many to pursue the thrilling and eerie world of ghost hunting. Yet, as we delve into this intriguing practice, we must shift our focus from merely seeking chills to rigorously pursuing truths. This transition elevates ghost hunting from a pastime to a serious scientific endeavor. As we approach the intricate subject of paranormal research, understanding its core principles and methodologies is essential.

This chapter aims to refine our perception of ghost hunting, highlighting it as a disciplined exploration rooted in science rather than just an adrenaline-fueled adventure.

The fascination with the paranormal often springs from deep-seated curiosity and the human desire to understand the unknown.

However, this exploration must be anchored in rationality and evidence-based practices. **Actual ghost hunting** involves a systematic approach where hypotheses are formed and tested, observations are documented meticulously, and conclusions are drawn soberly without the interference of bias or sensationalism.

Establishing a Scientific Foundation

As we explore further, it's imperative to define **the true purpose** of ghost hunting. It isn't simply about proving or disproving the existence of spirits but understanding anomalies through a scientific lens. By applying rigorous methods typically reserved for traditional fields of study—like controlled experiments and systematic observation—ghost hunting can be respected alongside more established scientific inquiries.

Beyond Thrills: The Pursuit of Knowledge

The distinction between thrill-seeking and genuine investigative pursuits is significant. While popular media often portrays ghost hunting as a spine-tingling entertainment form, its academic aspect is seldom highlighted. This chapter emphasizes transforming the perception of paranormal research from a hobby to a severe discipline, where findings contribute to broader scientific knowledge and understanding.

Cultivating Critical Thinking

Promoting scientific literacy and skepticism is essential to fostering a scientific community among paranormal enthusiasts.

Encouraging critical thinking helps debunk myths and focus on plausible explanations rather than accepting supernatural occurrences at face value. This not only aids in conducting more credible investigations but also educates others about interpreting such phenomena responsibly.

Reflecting on our journey through this book, we've tackled various aspects of ghost hunting—from understanding basic principles to debunking common myths and learning practical investigation techniques. Each step has been guided by a commitment to clarity, skepticism, and an evidence-based approach. By integrating these elements, readers are equipped with tools for investigation and a mindset geared toward rational inquiry.

This chapter serves as a guide and an inspiration for current and future generations of ghost hunters. Embracing change in this field means advocating for education and understanding mere entertainment. The transformation involves every enthusiast becoming a proponent of science, diligently dispelling fears rooted in misinformation.

We foster an informed community that values truth over sensation to pave the way for more reasoned discourse around paranormal topics. This enriches those directly involved in ghost hunting and enhances broader societal understanding of how we interpret unexplained phenomena, making us all more thoughtful observers of the world.

Ultimately, embracing scientific rigor does not strip away the intrigue of exploring the paranormal; instead, it adds depth to our understanding and ensures that our fascinations are grounded in reality rather than fantasy.

The Essence of Ghost Hunting as a Scientific Practice

Ghost hunting is not merely about chasing shadows in old buildings or seeking spectral encounters. It is a scientific endeavor to explore and explain phenomena that are not yet understood. True ghost hunters arm themselves with various scientific tools and methods, from EMF meters to digital voice recorders, approaching each investigation with a critical eye.

Imagine ghost hunting as if you were a detective in a mystery novel. The thrill lies not in the danger or the unknown per se but in piecing together clues, forming hypotheses, and ultimately solving the puzzle. Ghost hunting is about collecting data, analyzing it, and drawing conclusions based on evidence, not just personal experiences or feelings.

The discipline required in ghost hunting is akin to that in any scientific field. A ghost hunter must be patient, methodical, and unbiased, willing to observe and note every detail without jumping to conclusions. This approach ensures that the findings are reliable and that the investigations can be replicated, two pillars of any scientific endeavor.

In ghost hunting, embracing science means committing to continuous learning and improvement. Each investigation offers a chance to refine techniques, question assumptions, and deepen understanding of the unknown. This commitment to scientific rigor helps elevate ghost hunting from a hobby to a respected and valuable field of study.

The true purpose of ghost hunting is to explore the unexplained with the tools and mindset of science.

Thrills vs. Science in Paranormal Research

In paranormal research, it's easy to confuse thrill-seeking with genuine investigative pursuits. Thrill-seekers are drawn to ghost hunting for the adrenaline rush and the eerie stories they can share with friends. They relish the spooky atmosphere and the excitement of potentially encountering a ghost. However, their approach often needs more scientific rigor and primarily aims at entertainment.

In contrast, genuine paranormal investigators enter the field with a different mindset. They are akin to scholars, driven by a desire to understand and explain. These investigators use systematic methods to collect and analyze data, always aiming to rule out logical explanations before considering a paranormal cause. They maintain detailed logs, use technology effectively, and often collaborate with other experts to validate findings.

The difference between these two approaches can be illustrated with a simple analogy: thrill-seekers are like tourists snapping pictures of a monument, while genuine investigators are like archaeologists carefully excavating a site. The former seeks immediate gratification and is invested in long-term discovery and understanding.

This distinction is crucial in paranormal research, as the field is often criticized for its lack of scientific method. By promoting a more investigative approach, the community can gain credibility and produce findings that withstand scrutiny. This shift requires a change in attitude from the sensational to the empirical, focusing on evidence rather than anecdote.

Are we seeking mere thrills, or are we truly aiming to understand the boundaries of our reality?

Fostering Scientific Literacy and Skepticism

To elevate the field of ghost hunting, there is a pressing need to inspire scientific literacy and skepticism among paranormal enthusiasts. This goes beyond merely using scientific tools; it involves cultivating a mindset that questions, analyzes, and critically evaluates evidence.

Think of it like gardening. Just as a gardener nurtures plants, providing the right environment for growth, the ghost-hunting community must cultivate a culture where questioning and critical thinking are valued. This involves education and engagement, encouraging enthusiasts to think like scientists, skeptics, and researchers.

By promoting a more scientifically literate community, we can ensure that paranormal research is about exploring unknown phenomena and enhancing our understanding of science. This approach helps debunk myths, reduce fear, and foster a more rational appreciation of the unexplained.

By embracing scientific methods and critical thinking, we can transform ghost hunting from a pursuit of thrills to a disciplined exploration of the unknown, enriching both the field and its enthusiasts.

Through this book's journey, we've embarked on a transformative path from the murky shadows of myth to the clear light of understanding. Our final chapter not only seals this journey but propels us forward with a renewed vision for ghost hunting rooted firmly in science and critical thinking principles.

As we have discovered, ghost hunting is far more than a pursuit of spectral encounters; it's a disciplined scientific endeavor. This approach empowers us to sift through sensationalism, focusing on genuine phenomena with tools grounded in rationality. By applying scientific methodology, we elevate our pursuits from thrill-seeking to meaningful investigations that respect history and mystery.

Distinguishing between thrill-seeking and genuine investigative pursuits has allowed us to see paranormal research through a lens of integrity and purpose. This distinction must continue to inform the community's ethos, encouraging a deeper, more thoughtful engagement with the unknown.

Inspiring a culture of scientific literacy and skepticism is our most profound responsibility. It's about nurturing an environment where questioning is encouraged and evidence is king. This culture enhances our investigations and enriches our understanding of the world, allowing us to approach all claims with a healthy dose of skepticism.

As we close this book, remember that the path to mastering paranormal investigation is ongoing. The principles laid out here are just the beginning. I encourage you to keep questioning, learning, and, most importantly, keeping your curiosity alive.

Doing so will make you a better investigator and champion of truth in a field fraught with fiction.

Let this book be a beacon for all who seek to understand the unseen, guided by the light of reason and the spirit of inquiry.

Embrace these lessons and move forward confidently, knowing you contribute to a richer, more rational understanding of the paranormal. Together, we can continue to unveil the truth behind the mysteries that captivate our imaginations and challenge our knowledge.

Epilogue

Embracing the Shadows: A Journey Toward Understanding

As we draw the curtains on exploring the spectral and unexplained, we must reflect on our journey together. This book has been a compass through the foggy realms of paranormal claims, guiding you with a torch of skepticism and scientific inquiry. We delved into the mysteries that linger at the edges of our understanding.

Now, as we part ways, you are equipped with knowledge and a methodology to discern truth from fiction.

In your hands lies more than just a collection of pages; it's a toolkit for critical thinking, a shield against the allure of unsound sensationalism that often clouds the truth about paranormal phenomena. Whether you're whispering through ancient hallways or debunking eerie tales around a campfire, the insights from this book can transform how you interact with the world of mysteries.

We ventured through various hauntings and apparitions, dissected famous ghostly encounters, and scrutinized the tools and techniques used in paranormal investigations. The core takeaway is clear: **not everything that shimmers in the night is a ghost**, and not every bump in the dark demands a supernatural explanation.

For those inspired to take this further, whether in personal ventures or perhaps in educational settings, remember that skepticism is your foundation. Approach each claim with curiosity but also caution. Share these insights with peers or integrate them into community education programs. The ripple effect of informed knowledge is profound and far-reaching.

While I strive for thoroughness in every chapter, the realm of paranormal research is vast and ever-expanding. Areas such as digital spectral analysis or psychological affects of supposed hauntings beckon further scholarly exploration. I encourage you to contribute to these discussions—your unique observations could illuminate unseen corners of this enigmatic field.

Now is your moment to step forward, empowered by understanding and driven by an insatiable curiosity about what lies beyond the known. Let this book be your springboard into deeper inquiries and more enlightened discussions about the paranormal.

Let us part with a thought that resonates deeply within the heart of every seeker:

***"The important thing is not to stop questioning. Curiosity has its reason for existing."*—Albert Einstein.**

In this spirit, continue to question, explore, and uncover. The shadows await not with fear but with an invitation to understand their secrets.

Don't miss out!

Visit the website below and you can sign up to receive emails whenever Myrddin Sage publishes a new book. There's no charge and no obligation.

https://books2read.com/r/B-A-JBAOB-GWFBF

BOOKS 2 READ

Connecting independent readers to independent writers.

Did you love *Ghost Buster's Guide: The Truth Behind Paranormal Claims*? Then you should read *The Sword and the Sage: Unveiling the Truth of Excalibur and Merlin*[1] by Myrddin Sage!

[2]

Dive into the legendary world of King Arthur with "The Sword and the Sage: Unveiling the Truth of Excalibur and Merlin." This captivating book embarks on a quest to uncover the historical realities behind two of the most iconic figures in Arthurian legend: the mystical sword Excalibur and the enigmatic wizard Merlin.

Master the legends and discover the historical facts in weeks. This book is your comprehensive guide to separating myth from truth, providing a well-researched narrative that dismantles age-old myths and presents authentic stories rooted in history.

---

1. https://books2read.com/u/mg80l7

2. https://books2read.com/u/mg80l7

Excalibur: Explore the origins and significance of King Arthur's legendary sword. Learn how the tales of Excalibur have evolved over centuries and uncover the truths that inspired these enduring myths.

Merlin: Delve into the life and lore of Merlin, the wise and powerful wizard. From his mysterious birth to his role as Arthur's advisor, this book reveals the actual historical figures and events that shaped the legend of Merlin.

With meticulous research and engaging storytelling, "The Sword and the Sage" is perfect for history enthusiasts, Arthurian legend fans, and anyone eager to learn the truths behind the tales. No more myths—only truths await you in this enlightening journey through time.

Prepare to be enthralled by the revelations and insights offered in this definitive guide to Excalibur and Merlin. Embark on a historical adventure that will transform your understanding of these timeless legends.

Also by Myrddin Sage

Echoes of the Ancient: Unlocking the Mysteries of Celtic Myth

Mythic Japan: Unlocking the Legends of Gods and Heroes

Echoes of Enchantment: Navigating the Magic of Celtic Mythology

Warriors and Wizards: The Heroes of Celtic Myth

Echoes of Valhalla: Unveiling the Modern Wisdom of Norse Myths

Gods Among Us: The Power and Intrigue of Roman Mythology

The Sword and the Sage: Unveiling the Truth of Excalibur and Merlin

Myth Unleashed: Rediscovering the Legends of Hercules and the Pantheon

Echoes of the Gods: Rediscovering the Heroes and Deities of Ancient Egypt

Ancient Echoes: Embracing Egyptian Wisdom in Our Modern World

Alexander the Great Uncovered: A Journey Beyond the Battlefield

Ghost Buster's Guide: The Truth Behind Paranormal Claims

About the Author

At 67, Myrddin Sage steps into the spotlight as a newly published author, bringing a tapestry of rich life experiences and a vibrant imagination. His journey from a Navy Veteran to a Retired Dispatcher of Messengers has endowed him with profound insights into human cultures and the natural world. As Myrddin introduces his debut novel, he shares a narrative infused with wisdom, whimsy, and a deep respect for the interconnectedness of life. Drawing on his academic background and extensive travels, Myrddin's work explores themes of adventure, discovery, and the transformative power of knowledge. With his first publication, he proves that new chapters can be embarked upon at any stage of life, inspiring readers with the message that it is always the right time to follow one's passions.

www.ingramcontent.com/pod-product-compliance
Lightning Source LLC
Chambersburg PA
CBHW051241160726

47994CB00002B/979